Praying f...

D0245185

□ New Keswick Collection □

What He Says, Where He Sends, Philip Hacking

Praying for Others

Effective Intercession

by

Ronald Dunn

Marshall Pickering

Marshall Morgan and Scott
Marshall Pickering
34–42 Cleveland Street, London, W1P 5FB U.K.

Copyright © 1989 Ronald Dunn

First published in 1989 by Marshall Morgan and Scott Publications
Ltd. Part of the Marshall Pickering Holdings Group

British Library CIP Data
Dunn, Ronald
   Praying for others.
   1. Christian life. Prayer
   I. Title   II. Series
   248.3′2

ISBN: 0 551 01890 90

Text Set in Plantin by Prima Graphics, Camberley, Surrey
Printed in Great Britain by
Cox & Wyman Ltd, Reading, Berks

Contents

*This book is dedicated
to my father*
Cecil Dunn

and

to the memory of my mother
Eunice Bridges Dunn

Foreword

At Keswick we have had a long tradition of preachers from across the Atlantic who have won the hearts of Convention attenders. Amongst there Ron Dunn has a very special place. Not only at Keswick but at other conventions in Britain, his ministry has been much appreciated and has been multiplied endlessly through his tapes. It is therefore a great joy to have this book in our New Keswick Collection and Ron Dunn writes as he preaches.

There is a beautiful blend of illustration and strong biblical content. Exposition is illuminated by story and this particularly comes from a man with a deep pastoral heart and a wide experience of church ministry. The issues with which the author deals are very basic to Christian living and therefore we are very pleased to have this book in our new series. Prayer may not be in itself one of the great Keswick themes but the whole convention is steeped in prayer and the life of holiness very much begins at the place where we pray.

In reading the book it is important to understand that the light touch which is often there hides some very deep theological thinking about the whole subject of intercessory prayer. I believe that in our age we have rather lost out on intercession. We are almost pleased that we have got rid of the 'old-fashioned prayer meeting'. In the process I believe we have lost a great deal and if this book encourages people to start interceding more, both personally and with others, then it will achieve a great deal. In my book last year beginning this series, I spoke in terms of mission and service. How often that challenge has begun at the place of prayer and come to fruition because others have been praying for us.

As the author grapples with great problems which can arise when prayer does not seem to be answered, the reader will be led on spiritually. In an age when we always want instant answers we often become very immature. The saint who learns to pray may have deep agonies and much wrestling but he or she will get much close to the Lord himself. This book should do that for many of us and we are indebted to Ron Dunn for it.

Philip H. Hacking

Introduction

So I sought for a man among them who would make up a
   wall,
and stand in the gap before Me on behalf of the land,
that I should not destroy it;
but I found no one.

Ezekiel 22:30

A Christian never has to say, 'There's nothing I can do.'
We can do something. We can do something great, great
as Jesus did – even greater. We can pray.

Intercession – praying for others – is the secret
weapon of the kingdom of God. It is like a missile that
can be fired to any spot on earth, travel undetected at the
speed of thought and hit its target every time.

It can even be armed for delayed detonation. In his
prayer of John 17, Jesus said, 'I do not pray for these
alone, but also for those who will believe in me through
their word' (John 17:20). His prayer spans the centuries
and embraces all who have believed, or ever will believe.
Every time someone turns to Christ, the prayer of Jesus
is answered again: 2,000 years ago and still being
answered.

The implications are staggering. We, too, can pray
about things yet to happen, things, for instance, in the
lives of our children – and their children. We can wrap
them in the arms of intercession and march them through
the fires of hell and into the gates of heaven. This is the
inheritance we can leave our children – an inheritance
of prayer, prayers lifted to God long before they were
born, prayers answered long after we have gone.

There's more. Satan has no defence against this weapon;
he does not have an anti-prayer missile. The unbeliever

has many defences against our evangelistic efforts. He can refuse to attend church, and if he does attend, he can shift into neutral and count the cracks in the ceiling. You can go to his home, but he doesn't have to let you in. Hand him a tract on the street and he can throw it away. Get on television and he can switch channels. Call him on the phone and he can hang up. But he cannot prevent the Lord Jesus from knocking at the door of his heart in response to our intercession. People we cannot reach any other way, we can reach by way of the throne of grace.

But we do not intercede by default – because there is nothing else we can do. Some dismiss prayer as a weak alternative to practical action, an excuse for doing nothing. Offering to pray for someone is often nothing but a graceful way to excuse ourself from an awkward situation; it is an exit line.

It is true that we should do more than pray. It is also true that there is nothing *more* we can do than pray, because intercession is the heart of redemption. Speaking of the Suffering Servant who was to come, Isaiah said, 'He made intercession for the transgressors' (Isaiah 53:12). For Christ intercession was more than praying. His birth was part of the intercession; his life on earth, his public ministry, his teaching, his miracles, his agony in the garden, his scourging, the mocking and the shame, that awful dying on the cross – all this was intercession. For him, becoming a man was an act of intercession.

That has not changed. The work of redemption is still the work of intercession. Jesus is interceding, the Holy Spirit is interceding, and we share in that intercession because God has made us a kingdom of priests (1 Peter 2:9; Revelation 1:6).

Intercessors have influence in high places. As God prepared to bring judgment upon the cities of Sodom and Gomorrah, he said, 'Shall I hide from Abraham what I am doing?' (Genesis 18:17). When God was angry with Israel, 'He said that he would destroy them, had not

Moses his chosen one stood before him in the breach to turn away his wrath, lest he destroy them' (Psalm 106:23).

God has always sought intercessors, someone to stand in the gap before him for the sake of the land. But he has always had a hard time finding them. In Ezekiel's day God looked for a man to stand in the breach that sin had made between God and Israel. But he found no one. Isaiah tells us that God looked for a man, but found no one and wondered that there was no intercessor (Isaiah 59: 16). Today, God is still looking for people to stand in the gap.

In 1972, the church I pastored launched a twenty-four-hour, seven-days-a-week intercessory prayer ministry. God had been awakening us to prayer for some time. Throughout the week clusters of people gathered to pray during lunch hours or early evenings. I preached for three months on intercessory praying, climaxed by the inauguration of the prayer ministry. We did not organise to create a prayer ministry – we organised a ministry already created.

The intercessory prayer ministry revolutionised the lives of many who were prayed for, and revolutionised, I believe, the lives of those who did the praying. Other churches and Christian organisations asked for help to start prayer ministries of their own.

Of course, there had to be a book. I finished the first draft in 1973 – and laid it aside for fifteen years.

Then followed some 'years of living dangerously', times of crisis in which everything I had preached was challenged. I found that what I had preached was true – I had just preached it too easily. I'm glad I waited till now to finish the book.

Some acknowledgments are in order: Joanne Gardner, my secretary since 1966, spent many long hours transcribing the original tapes. I am indebted to those precious intercessors of MBBC, who with me, learned how to get bread for hungry travellers. I'm grateful to my son,

Stephen, and my daughter, Kimberly, for their permission – permission I'm sure they would have given had I asked (it's easier to get forgiveness than permission) – to drag them in as illustrations. I'm indebted to Stephen for his help in gathering and organising material. And, as always, to my wife, Kaye, for her uncountable kindnesses and her unaccountable love and for reading and rereading the manuscript with a loving but lethal eye that tries to keep my writing honest.

To punctuate his words that 'men always ought to pray and not lose heart' (Luke 18:1), Jesus told a parable about an unjust judge and an unfortunate widow. It is the story of a judge who neither feared God nor regarded man, and a widow who came to him seeking justice. Naturally, she had no influence, no money, nothing to make it profitable to the judge to vindicate her. But the widow was stubbornly persistent and the judge said, 'Though I do not fear God nor regard man, yet because this widow troubles me I will avenge her, lest by her continual coming she weary me' (Luke 18:5).

The meaning is obvious: we always ought to pray and never lose heart. And then Jesus said, 'Nevertheless, when the Son of Man comes, will he really find faith on the earth?' (Luke 18:8). The construction of the question implies a negative answer: not likely.

But it is a certain kind of faith that Jesus will be looking for when he returns. In the Greek text, 'faith' carries a definite article that points to a specific kind of faith, literally, '*this* kind of faith'. When Jesus returns, will he find on earth the kind of faith that prays without ceasing, faith like that of the widow who refused to lose heart and by her 'continual coming' seized the prize?

God has always looked for intercessors. When Jesus comes back he will still be looking for that kind of faith. This book is sent out with the prayer that when he comes, he will find some of us 'standing in the gap'.

1: The Jesus Secret

Around midnight, on the eve of his death, Jesus led his small band of disciples through the streets of Jerusalem and out through the city's eastern gate. Crossing the Kedron, he brought them to a favourite hideaway of his at the foot of Mount Olivet, the garden of Gethsemane.

On the way to the garden, Jesus had continued the ominous discourse begun in the upper room. It had been an unsettling evening for the disciples; they were bewildered by the strange behaviour of Judas, and the cryptic conversation between him and Jesus. Even Jesus had been 'troubled in his spirit'. He was talking in riddles; he spoke of leaving them, and something about his Father's house. They tried to understand but it was difficult. The more Jesus told them, the more confused they became.

'If you had known me,' Jesus said, 'you would have known my Father also; and from now on you know him and have seen him' (John 14:7).

Philip broke the silence of the disciples: 'Lord, show us the Father, and it is sufficient for us.'

Philip seized upon Jesus' words about the Father. Give us a more definite word, he seemed to be saying, give us an unquestionable vision. Let us see not by faith only, but also by sight. That would be enough, even if Jesus left them.

In his answer Jesus disclosed the secret of his life and work, which would soon become the secret of their life and work. He said, 'He who has seen me has seen the

Father . . .. Do you not believe that I am in the Father, and the Father in me? The words that I say to you I do not speak on my own authority; but the Father who dwells in me does the works. Believe me that I am in the Father and the Father in me, or else believe me for the sake of the works themselves' (John 14:9–11).

Philip said, 'Show us the Father,' as though he had neer seen him. But he had seen him, he just didn't know he had. Every time he watched Jesus heal a leper, he saw the Father; every time he listened to Jesus teach, he was hearing the Father. But it really did look as though Jesus was doing those things; it sounded like him, too. Philip was confused.

By his answer, Jesus was saying, 'I am not the source of my own sufficiency. The things that I said and did – they did not initiate with me. I did nothing on my own. It was the Father.' Jesus disclaimed any credit for his words or his works. Both were those of his Father who dwelt in him.

Jesus was not the source of his own power. This helps us understand what he meant when he said, 'Most assuredly, I say to you, the Son can do nothing of himself, but what he sees the Father do; for whatever he does, the Son also does in like manner' (John 5:19). And again in verse 30: 'I can of myself do nothing. As I hear, I judge; and my judgment is righteous, because I do not seek my own will but the will of the Father who sent me.'

The secret surfaces again in John 8:28: 'Then Jesus said to them, "When you lift up the Son of Man, then you will know that I am he, and that I do nothing of myself; but as my Father taught me, I speak these things.'

And again: 'For I have not spoken on my own authority; but the Father who sent me gave me a command, what I should say and what I should speak' (John 12:49).

A few moments later Jesus would say to his disciples, 'I will not leave you orphans' (John 14:18). That was exactly what they were afraid of – being left like helpless orphans. They couldn't bear the thought that he might leave them, which late he had talked about a lot. Every time Jesus brought up the cross, they tried to change the subject. They must have thought, 'We've been such a failure with him, what will we be without him?'

But listen to Jesus: 'I am not the source of my own sufficiency. The explanation of the miracles I worked and the words I spoke is not found in Me. The explanation lies with the Father. He did it; he did it through me, but he did it.

'Listen to me, Philip. The secret of the works is not my physical *presence*. And if the secret is not my physical presence, then my physical *absence* won't make any difference.

'As a matter of fact, if you will just trust me, the works that I have done, you will continue to do, and you will do even greater works than these.

'You think my leaving will ruin my work and make it more difficult for you. But my elevation to the right hand of God will enable you to do through my intercession greater works than I have done. My presence in heaven and the Spirit's presence in you is the pledge of greater power and greater works'.

'The redemptive purpose of God will not miss a beat when I leave. You will pick it up before it touches the ground and carry it on . . .

'As the Father dwelt in me and did the works, so he will dwell in you and do the works through you. And not the Father only, but I also will come to dwell in you.'

The Lord was leaving, but his departure would not dismantle his work. As the Father had worked through the Son, he would work through the disciples.

This was the basis for the extraordinary promise he gave them – and us. 'Most assuredly, I say to you, he who believes in me, the works that I do he will do also; and greater works than these he will do, because I go to my Father' (John 14:12). I say 'and us', because the promise is to 'he who believes in me', and that's us.

To those who believe in him, Jesus promised two things: one, they will *equal* his works, and, two, they will *exceed* his works. And fifty days later, in the very city where the Lord was crucified, the disciples did both. After ten days in the upper room, the disciples emerged with the power of the Holy Spirit upon them, and after a short sermon by Peter, 3,000 people were added to the church.

And as long as I can remember, we've been trying to do it again, but the Pentecostal power continues to elude us. I don't know of many Christians who would be willing to say that the church is living up to the promise of John 14:12. So the question is, why not?

To answer that question we must first understand what Jesus meant by *greater works*.

Perhaps the real key is found in the phrase we often overlook: 'because I go to my Father'. Jesus makes it clear that the promise of greater works can be fulfilled only if he returns to his Father. Why? Why was it necessary to ascend to the Father before the disciples could realise this promise? The ascension was certainly not essential to the working of physical miracles. Jesus had been doing that for three years.

But this new thing Jesus is talking about demands that he first ascend to the Father. He is evidently speaking of something new, something on a higher level, something in a new dimension. The promise cannot refer to a mere continuation or even acceleration of what had already been going on for three years.

Upon ascending, Jesus would send the Spirit (John 7: 39, 16:7) and occupy the place of intercessor to hear and answer the prayers of his disciples. It was this that would make possible the doing of greater works.

Jesus is emphasising the union that will exist between them although they will be separated physically. He is going away but he will remain with them, and if they trust him, the work that he started will continue and even increase. His physical absence will not diminish the work – it will enhance it. In other words, when they work, it will be Jesus working still; his works will be their works and their works, his. Barnabas Lindars says, 'As their works are the works of Jesus, they will be just as much the activity of God in the world as his own acts were.'[1]

'Works' and 'greater works' refer not so much to the independent and specific acts of the disciples, but rather to the fact that everything they do will actually be Jesus doing it through them.

The 'greater works' of the disciples depends upon the 'going' of Jesus. His ascension will mean the descent of the empowering Holy Spirit and the inauguration of Christ's heavenly intercession, thus enabling the church to fulfil its mission of evangelising the world. For as J.C.Ryle pointed out, '"Greater works" mean more conversions. There is no greater work possible than the conversion of a soul.'[2]

> What Jesus means we may see in the narratives of the Acts. There are a few miracles of healing, but the emphasis is on the mighty works of conversion. On the day of Pentecost alone more believers were added to the little band of believers than throughout Christ's entire earthly life. There we see a literal fulfilment of 'greater works than these shall be done'. During His lifetime the Son of God was confined in His influence to a comparatively small sector of Palestine. After His depature His followers were able to work in widely scattered places and influence much larger numbers of men.[3]

Which brings us back to the question of why a great

9

part of today's church is not living up to the promise of greater works.

The best place to find the answer is in the promise itself. How did Jesus intend us to realise that promise? The pledge of greater works in verse 12 is followed by another in verse 13: 'And whatever you ask in my name, that will I do, that the Father may be glorified in the Son.'

Notice that verse 13 starts with 'And'. A grand old preacher once told me, 'Don't ever take as a complete text any verse that starts with "and" because it isn't complete.' 'And' at the beginning of a sentence lets us know that what we are about to read is a continuation of, or a completion of, the thought of the preceding sentence. This is not the 'and' of a writer moving to another subject; this is the 'and' of a speaker continuing his thought.

'. . . the works that I do he will do also; and greater works than these he will do, because I go to my Father. *And* whatever you ask in my name that I will do . . .' (Emphasis added).

The greater works of verse 12 are to be accomplished by the believing prayer of verse 13. It is through prayer tha we equal and exceed his works. The book of Acts is filled with prayer meetings; prayer surrounded every forward thrust of the infant church. Take another look at the believers gathered at Pentecost. They prayed ten days, preached ten minutes and 3,000 people were saved. Today we pray ten minutes, preach ten days and are ecstatic if anyone is saved.

But remember, Jesus said we would do it the way he did it; his secret would become our secret. Did Jesus pray much? Was it a conspicuous part of his life? If Jesus could say and do only what he heard and saw the Father do, he had to spend a lot of time listening and seeing. And he did. There was a recognisable rhythm in the life of Jesus: he would withdraw to meditate, then go out to minister. Again and again this pattern repeats itself. The public life of Jesus was supported by his private life with the Father. He had a secret history.

Prayer is the secret. It was the way of Jesus, the way of the early church and it should be the way of the church now.

But for all the reverence that surrounds it, prayer suffers from a poor image. We tend to think of it as something the women do, something for the weak and more delicate saints to engage in while those-who-get-the-job-done are up and doing.

We all have our private images of prayer. Mine, which I've had since I was a kid, is of a little Spanish mission in the desert, with a monk with a tonsured haircut standing in front of it. He is wearing a coarse brown robe (it looks hot) girded with a length of rope. His hands are clasped prayerfully together; he appears meek and fragile, unworldly, unsophisticated and undernourished (from fasting, probably). He stands there gazing up at the Lone Ranger and Tonto, their steeds straining at their reins, flared nostrils snorting, legs dancing amid exploding clouds of dust. The Lone Ranger and Tonto (pure in heart, hence, unafraid) have drawn their guns and their faces are fixed in grim determination.

The monk says something about going with them.

'You are a brave man, Father,' the masked man says. 'But it may be dangerous. You had better stay here where it is safe.'

'But I want to help,' says the monk.

The strong yet kind eyes of the masked man fasten on the eyes of the monk: 'You can pray.' Suddenly the great white horse rears up on its hind legs, and with a wave of his hat and a hearty 'Heigh Ho Silver – Awaaaay!' the Lone Ranger and his faithful companion gallop off to the danger that awaits them.

The camera of my imagination does not follow the priest into the mission to watch him pray. It chases after

11

the Lone Ranger and Tonto. That's where the action is.

I remember speaking to a group of church leaders in Honolulu. They had invited me to speak specifically on prayer and how to develop an intercessory prayer ministry in the local church. I told them that the church had programmes for everything else – visitation, witnessing, discipleship, stewardship – but few churches had a prayer programme. I told them that this seemed ironic considering the great emphasis the Bible placed upon prayer.

After a morning session, one of the delegates, a director of a denominational evangelism department, tapped me on the shoulder, gave me a conspiratorial wink and drew me aside.

'You know,' he said in a soft voice, 'I think this prayer thing is a great idea. But I'm afraid it could get out of hand.'

'What do you mean?'

'Well,' he said, 'People could get so involved in praying they wouldn't do anything.'

When I realised the man was serious, I assured him that I had yet to come across a church that was praying so much they had to be told to slack off. We would just have to cross that bridge when we came to it. So far, we haven't come to it.

Prayer is not a substitute for work, nor is it merely preparation for work. Prayer *is* work. It is hard work.

And this is the other side of prayer's poor image, the image of ancient saints kneeling on cold stone floors in the dark hours of winter mornings, crying long to the Lord. Prayer is serious business, they seem to say to us; there is no room for foolishness here. To do it right requires rigorous discipline.

Prayer is the most intimidating word in the Christian vocabulary. We've all been daunted by the pronouncements of old saints like Martin Luther, who said, 'I have so much to do today that I shall spend the first three hours in prayer,' and the stories of prayer warriors like Praying Hyde of India or David Brainerd who prayed in knee-deep snow so long and vigorously the snow around him melted, and who caught pneumonia and died. Not to forget the apostle James who, according to tradition, was called 'camel knees'. He spent so much time praying his knees resembled the calloused knees of a camel.

The hallowed ghosts of these ancestors have dumped piles of guilt on all of us. I suspect most of us have had a go at the four a.m. ritual – rising a great while before day to 'wrestle with God in prayer'.

'No pain, no gain,' appears to be the motto of prayer. I've never really understood why prayer had to be a test of physical endurance. I much prefer the prayer-lunch to the prayer-breakfast.

Granted this picture of prayer has been overdone. But in the attempt to correct the misconception and expunge the guilt it creates, we have overreacted. Some have so drastically redefined prayer to fit our jazzed-up stream-lined lives, that it turns out we have been praying all along and didn't know it ('Being aware of our riches in Christ is true prayer').

And so we knock any talk about prayer being hard work, requiring personal sacrifice, blood, sweat and tears. But only when we say it about prayer. Sacrifice, hard work and pain are admired in a twenty-six-mile marathon for Muscular Dystrophy; in prayer they are ridiculed.

Despite the fact that we have grown up with exaggerated ideas of prayer, it remains true that prayer is work. Throughout the New Testament prayer is pictured as a struggle, a fight, as hand-to-hand combat. When Herod cast Peter into prison, we are told that 'constant prayer was offered to God for him by the church' (Acts 12:5). 'Constant' is the translation of a Greek word that means to stretch out, to push yourself to the limit of endurance.

Paul pleaded with the Christians at Rome 'that you *strive* together with me in your prayers to God for me'

(Romans 15:30; emphasis added). Literally, Paul is saying, 'Agonise with me in prayer'. The word means to struggle or fight; it is a picture of wrestling in prayer and it was exactly what Epaphras, a co-worker of Paul's was doing for the Colossians – he was 'labouring fervently' in prayer (Colossians 4:12).

In the same letter, Paul advises the Colossians to 'Continue earnestly in prayer, being vigilant in it' (Colossians 4:2). 'Continue' is made of two words, 'to be strong', and 'towards', calling us to stick to our praying, to persist in it. Two attitudes are to mark our praying: diligence and vigilance. Paul has a good reason for cautioning his readers to be vigilant, to be alert, to pray 'with their eyes wide open'. A consistent prayer life is hard to build up and even harder to maintain. There is nothing that we are so easily turned away from as prayer; in an overcrowded schedule, prayer is usually the first thing to go.

To make prayer palatable to modern-day Christians do we have to make it incompatible with the New Testament kind? 'Mysterious as it is,' writes Curtis Mitchell, 'persistent struggle is a vital part of New Testament prayer. Lose the importunity of prayer, reduce it to simply conferring with God, lose the real sense of conflict, lose the habit of wrestling and the hope of prevailing, make prayer mere walking with God in friendly talk and, precious as it is, you tend to forfeit the reality of prayer in the end. In actuality, you make prayer mere conversation instead of the soul's great action. There is an inexplicable element of dogged struggle in biblical praying.'[4]

Prayer is the secret of Jesus, and he has passed it on to us. But not all Christians receive it. The secret of greater works is received only by those who say, '*I believe God will do his greatest works through my prayer.*'

A number of years ago, Alan Redpath, former pastor of Moody Memorial Church in Chicago and a man greatly used of God around the world, suffered a severe stroke. Afterwards while he was convalescing, he said, 'I believe the Lord has taught me this lesson above all: *Never to undertake more Christian work than can be covered in believing prayer*. Each of us has to work out what this means in personal experience in relation to our ministry, but I believe it is an abiding principle for us all. To fail here is not to act in faith but in presumption.'[5]

And that is the Jesus Secret.

2: Greater Works Than These

In one way or another, to one god or another, man has always prayed. He has always been devoured by the need of something outside himself, beyond his reach, something spiritual or supernatural, a place to run to, someone to cry out to, someone who takes notice of his predicament. He longs to escape the sense of crushing fate, the feeling that all things are fixed and unalterable. Prayer is more than a religious exercise, it is a human necessity.

Prayer and the Christian life are synonymous. To say that I am a Christian is the same as saying, I pray. 'For what is prayer? To connect every thought with the thought of God. To look on everything as His appointment. To submit every thought, wish and resolve to Him. To feel His presence, so that it shall restrain us even in our wildest joy.'[1]

As we saw in the previous chapter, Jesus revealed that the church would do greater works than he had done. 'Most assuredly, I say to you, he who believes in me, the works that I do he will do also; and greater works than these shall he do, because I go to my Father' (John 14:12). And these greater works, he said, would be done through prayer.

So astonishing were these words that Jesus repeated them – as though he saw incredulity flash across their faces. 'Yes, I repeat it, anything you ask for as bearers of my name I will do it for you' (John 14:14, Williams).

As a matter of fact during this last meeting with his disciples before his death (John 14–17), Jesus repeated these words six times: 'If you ask . . . I will do.' Dr Curtis Mitchell writes, 'In this simple statement, prayer is set forth as the *primary human factor in the accomplishment of God's program on earth.* With a startling boldness, Christ asserted that divine action, in some mysterious manner, is conditioned upon believing prayer. Thus prayer is set forth as the chief task of the believer. It is *his* responsibility to ask. It is God's responsibility to accomplish.'[2]

If I had to pick one verse in the Bible that most adequately and concisely defines prayer, it would be John 14:13: 'And whatever you ask in my name, that I will do, that the Father may be glorified in the Son.'

In Chapter One we saw Christ's promise of greater works. Now let's examine the kind of praying by which these works are done; just some basic principles and illustrations. We'll slice this verse like a loaf of bread, and the first slice is:

'*Whatever you ask*'

Whatever sets the boundary of prayer. A man in our church came to my office one day to talk about a serious business problem. When I asked him if he had prayed about it he looked offended and said, 'Of course not.'

'Why not?' I asked.

'That's business,' he said. 'I couldn't pray about that.'

To my visitor prayer was 'For Official Use Only,' 'official' meaning 'religious'. But in prayer everything is considered official business. To the question, 'For what may I pray?' Jesus answers, 'Whatever'. 'If you abide in me, and my words abide in you, you will ask what you desire, and it shall be done for you' (John 15:7). The Bible encourages us to pray about everything.

When speaking of prayer, the Bible uses big, limitless words. For example, Jeremiah 33:3: 'Call unto me, and I will answer you, and show you great and mighty things, which you do not know.' The phrase 'mighty things' literally means 'things that are hidden, inaccessible, fenced in.' Prayer knocks down the fences. Nothing lies

17

beyond the reach of prayer; there are no boundaries to its jurisdiction.

Prayer is always relevant. If a thing's big enough to worry about, it's big enough to pray about. Whatever is a concern in the heart of man is a concern in the heart of God.

Worry about nothing, Paul said, and pray about everything (Philippians 4:6). 'Nothing – Everything.' Prayer touches both ends of our lives and covers everything between.

The second phrase of our prayer verse is

in my Name.

'Whatever you ask in my name.' In these upper room chapters (John 14–16) Jesus uses this phrase several times.

'Whatever you ask in my name' (John 14:13).

'If you ask anything in my name' (John 14:14).

'Whatever you ask of the Father in my name' (John 15:16).

'If you ask the Father for anything, he will give it to you in my name' (John 16:23).

'Until now you have asked for nothing in my name; ask and you will receive' (John 16:24).

'In that day you will ask in my name' (John 16:26).

With these words, *in my name,* Jesus signals a new stage in his redemptive work and a new dimension in his relationship with the disciples. He had promised them that they would do greater works 'because I go to my Father'. Until he ascended to the Father, his redemptive work was incomplete; only when he had sat down at the right hand of the majesty on high would the promises be realised. Having by himself made purification for our sins, he is become the mediator, the executor of his own testament. He has taken up the reins of authority.

'He sat down' – a work ended and a work begun. The work of the cross, his shame, suffering and sacrifice finished. The work of the throne, intercession and mediation begun. It is through Jesus that men now come to God. No longer in the name of sacrifices, but in the name of the Sacrifice. No longer through the mediation of earthly priests, but now through our Great High Priest who has entered into heaven, there to appear in the presence of God for us.

To make up for his physical absence Jesus promised the disciples three things: his peace (John 14:27); the Paraclete (John 14:16), and prayer in his name (John 16:23,24). Praying 'in the name of Jesus' is a totally new teaching on prayer and is found only in the Gospel of John.

What is so special about this – this praying in Jesus' name? And not only praying in his name, but *living* in his name.

Paul instructs that whatever we do 'in word or in deed, do all in the name of the Lord Jesus, giving thanks to the Father through him' (Colossians 3:17).

The name of Jesus is not a secret code that works some kind of magic spell when it is invoked, like 'Open Sesame!', or 'Shazam!' It isn't a tool to be manipulated. To pray in the name of Jesus means to pray 'by the authority of', 'in harmony with', or 'sanctioned by'. Christ has given us the right to pray in his name because we are his representatives, and we ask as his representatives because we are about his business.

Jesus is totally identified with his name. His name signifies *what* he is and *what* he has done. In Luke 9:48 Jesus said, 'Whoever receives this little child in my name receives me, and whoever receives me receives him that sent me.' To receive someone in Jesus' name is like receiving Jesus himself. To recognise his name means to recognise what and who he is.

Let's look, for example, at Romans 10:13, 'For whoever calls upon the name of the Lord shall be saved.' This is a part of 'The Roman Road to Salvation'. I've used it many times witnessing to lost people. But the verse says much more than, 'If you call on Christ to save you, he will.' That's true – he will. But Paul's statement isn't restricted to prayer. The verb *call* used here is first, acclamation, and then invocation.[3]

To 'call on the name of the Lord,' is to acknowledge that Jesus is what his name says he is: Lord. This verse is saying the same thing as verse 9: 'If you confess with your mouth, Jesus is Lord ['call on the name of the Lord', verse 13] and believe in your heart that God has raised him from the dead, you will be saved.' His name is 'Lord' and he is what his name says he is – Lord. And all who acknowledge him as Lord (call on his name) will be saved.

Now let's gather it all together. To pray or act in the name of Jesus means that we do so by his authority, with his approval, and that what we pray or do is consistent with his character as expressed in his name. You can't lie or steal 'in Jesus' name'; that is inconsistent with his nature. He would never grant you authority to use his name in that setting.

To pray in the name of Jesus, then, is to pray 'according to his will'; that is, what we are asking for has his approval, is consistent with his nature, character and purpose, and, therefore, it is as though Jesus himself were making the request – 'this is what Jesus would ask'. That is our authority.

When Peter and John healed the crippled man at the Beautiful gate of the Temple, Peter said to him, 'In the name of Jesus Christ of Nazareth, rise up and walk' (Acts 3:6). The crowd of people who constantly thronged the temple area were 'filled with wonder and amazement at what had happened to him,' and they ran towards Peter and John. And when 'Peter saw it, he responded to the people: "Men of Israel, why do you marvel at this . . . as though by our own power or godliness we had made this man walk?"' (Acts 3:12). The power to heal was not a prize awarded to them because they were godly. 'His

20

name, through faith in his name, has made this man strong' (Acts 3:16).

God does not welcome us to the throne of grace because of what we have done, but because of what Christ has done. We come in Jesus' name. And the Father receives us in his name.

Here's a little experiment that might nail down this truth for you. The next time you pray, tell God you are coming to Him in your own name, and that you demand to be heard because of your own righteousness. You will beat a quick retreat back to Jesus.

God sent me some more light in a surprising way. We were in Arkansas visiting my brother and his family, and the county fair was in full swing. One night we loaded everybody into the car and went to the fair. We weren't there long when it became obvious our children were not interested in the Blue Ribbon hogs and the award-winning cows. They wanted to get on to the carnival and the rides. So, abandoning the more cultural aspects of the fair, we headed for the carnival and candy floss.

All the rides were ten cents a piece. We bought a big roll of red ten-cent tickets and got organised. At the time my brother had one child, Rebecca; I had three – Ron Jr., Steve and Kimberly. I positioned myself at the entrance of the rides and as the kids came by, holding our their hands, I tore off a red ten-cent ticket and gave it to them.

I was standing at the entrance to the Tilt-A-Whirl with the roll of tickets. First, Rebecca came by, holding out her hand and I gave her a ticket. Then Kimberly came by with her hand out and I gave her a ticket; Ronnie was next and then Stephen, holding out their hands for a red ten-cent ticket.

And right behind Steve comes a little boy I've never seen in my life – holding out his hand for a red ten-cent ticket. Who is this kid? What's he up to? Those tickets cost ten cents a piece – you don't go around giving them to every little kid with his hand out. The boy stood there, hand outstretched, waiting. I ignored him; he stood there; the line behind him piled up. Would-be Tilt-A-Whirl riders grew restless and demand to know what was holding things up. Then Steve turns around, points to the importunate little beggar and says, 'Dad, he's my friend. I told him you would give him a ticket.'

Friend? We hadn't been there twenty minutes. I looked down. The boy was still standing there, hand outstretched. Do you know what I did? I tore off a red ten-cent ticket and gave it to him – not because I wanted to, but because my son told this boy that his dad would give him a ticket. I'm not about to embarrass my son or make a liar of him. Though he didn't realise it, the little boy was asking for a ticket 'in Stephen's name', and I gave him a ticket 'in Stephen's name'. I made good Stephen's word.

And standing at the entrance of the Tilt-A-Whirl with a roll of red ten-cent tickets, I thought: Yes, that's it. I go to the Father and say, 'YourSon said that if I ask for a red ten-cent ticket, you will give me one.' I ask in Jesus' name and the Father gives in Jesus' name. The Father makes good the word of the Son.

The third slice:

'And what you ask, that will I do.'

In the following verse Jesus repeats the promise: 'If you ask me anything in my name, *I will do it*. You ask, says Jesus, and I will act. He doesn't say, 'I will *help* you do it'; he says, '*I* will do it.'

Go back to verse 12 where Jesus says that 'he who believes . . . the works that I do shall he do also . . . and greater works than these shall he do.' In one verse Jesus says that *we* will do great works, then in the next verse he says, '*I* will do it'. Who does the works – Christ or us?

Both Jesus and we do the works. Remember our discussion of verses eight through ten in the last chapter? When Philip asked Jesus to show them the Father, Jesus said that if they had seen him, they had seen the Father. 'Do you not believe that I am in the Father, and the Father in me? The words that I say to you I do not speak on my own initiative, but the Father abiding in me does his works.'

When Philip and the others saw Jesus work and heard him speak, they were actually hearing and seeing the Father speak and work, for the things Jesus did were really the works of the Father who dwelt in him. To one who didn't know better, it looked as if it were Jesus speaking and working. But it was, in fact, the Father acting through the Son.

And what was true of the Father and the Son is true of us also. We do great and greater works but it is actually Jesus doing them through us – in response to our believing prayer. We often say, earth waits for heaven to act, but it can also be said that heaven waits for earth to ask.

I don't play tennis much any more; I wasn't ever very good, but I was always open to anything that could help me. One day watching a match on TV, I saw a commercial advertising the Wilson T-2000 metal racket. It showed Jimmy Connors making a lot of fancy shots while a hidden narrator said, 'The Wilson T-2000. The only metal racket to ever win both Wimbledon and Forest Hills.'

So that was my problem! All this time I had played with a wooden Dunlop Maxply. If the Wilson T-2000 could win Wimbledon and Forest Hills, it could certainly handle my little games. Well, I played with one all summer long. I don't remember winning a single match; my game didn't improve. I concluded that the Wilson Sporting Company was guilty of false advertising.

The truth is, the Wilson T-2000 didn't win Wimbledon and Forest Hills. Jimmy Connors did – using a Wilson T-2000. When the fans walked away from the match they didn't talk about what a great racket the Wilson T-2000 was. They talked about how great Jimmy Connors was.

Now a tennis racket is essential. Even Jimmy Connors couldn't win without a racket. But it isn't the racket that wins, it's the champion who wins, using the racket. And in the doing of great and greater works, we are the racket through which Jesus does them.

How significant is prayer? Only this: there are some things God will do if we ask him, that he will not do if we don't ask him. There are some things God will not do unless we ask him to. The words of Jesus, 'If you ask, I will do,' carry the obvious implication that if we do not ask, Jesus will not act. James says it plainly enough: 'You do not have because you do not ask' (James 4:2).

Here is a surprising fact about the healing miracles recorded in the Gospels. Jesus rarely took the initiative in those miracles. Ordinarily, Jesus did not heal someone unless they asked him to. And sometimes they almost had to chase him down. Bartimaeus cried so long and loud before Jesus stopped to listen, the crowd was telling the blind beggar to shut up (Mark 10:46–52). Jesus ignored, then insulted the Syrophoenician woman before healing her daughter (Matthew 15:21–28). Jairus took the initiative and came to Jesus on behalf of his daughter; the woman with the issue of blood touched Jesus before he noticed her.

At this point we could raise a lot of knotty questions – questions like, Does God change his mind? or, Is God's will a will of decree or a will of desire? Or both? Or neither? I'm disinclined to chase after questions like that lest we get bogged down in speculation and never get around to praying. If we wait until we understand everything about prayer and how it works, we'll never pray. Vance Havner used to say, 'I don't understand all about electricity, but I'm not going to sit around in the dark till I do.' We don't have to understand prayer to pray.

Whatever our answer to these questions might be it must (1) leave God's sovereignty intact, and (2) leave us where we have to trust him. Suffice to say that God speaks to us in language we can understand, and God's word to us is, *he responds to our prayers*. That is the way he said it and that is the way we are to take it.

Now, one more slice. All this, Jesus says, is in order that

'The Father may be glorified in the Son.'

Here is the supreme motive of all praying. The chief end of prayer is not that we may get what we ask for, but that God may be glorified in the getting of it. This is the plumbline we will return to again and again in this book – the glory of God.

This is the second of what I call 'The Big Three' that we have met in this chapter. By 'The Big Three' I mean the three qualifiers of all prayer. Every petition is formed within the context of these three provisions: the will of God, the glory of God, and the name of Jesus. These are the Big Three, and yet they are one, for whatever is the will of God is also for the glory of God. And nothing done in the name of Jesus would be contrary to God's will or inconsistent with his glory. So it is correct to say that I can pray in the name of Jesus only when what I'm asking for is according to the will of God, and the answer will bring glory to God.

'That the Father may be glorified in the Son.' When my motive for asking is the same as his for answering, I'm on praying ground. When I want what he wants, we're in business.

I think God delights in prayer because when he does something by answering prayer, there is no doubt that he is the one who has done it. We Christians have a knack for giving God the glory while taking the credit for ourselves. In describing some great accomplishment, we share in glorious detail how diligently we planned and studied and surveyed and planned even more, how hard and long we laboured to bring about this wonderful thing. But we are careful to add this postscript: 'to God be the glory,' as though we were tipping a waiter. We take all the credit and give God all the glory. But when God works in obvious answer to prayer, he gets both the credit and the glory.

In my last pastorate our youth choir was invited one summer to participate in a citywide evangelistic crusade in Salt Lake City, Utah. They would perform in shopping malls and parks during the day and in the crusade services at night. Everybody was excited. But we had 4,000 problems, and every one of them had a picture of George Washington on it. The trip would cost 4,000 dollars and we didn't have it.

Someone suggested we raise the money and in some moment of sublime unconsciousness I agreed to let the young people stage a pancake supper. I've always hated things like that – you know, buy a pancake and lend a hand to God who has fallen on hard times – that kind of stuff.

At any rate, we chose a Saturday and printed a hundred tickets and sold pancakes. I will never forget that Saturday morning, the morning I recovered from my fit of unconsciousness, and the sight that greeted my eyes. Our church was next to a hamburger shack called WhatAburger; they made huge hamburgers and when you saw one you were supposed to say, 'What a burger!' Our church marquee yelled, 'WhatApancake! WhatA-church!' The young people were standing in the middle of the busy street, wearing chef hats WhatAburger had given them, with placards hawking pancakes hanging around their necks, flagging down cars, imploring the drivers to stop for a pancake.

I parked my car and, with my head down, looking neither to the left nor to the right, I stepped quickly into the church. There, standing in the foyer, wearing silly-looking chef hats from WhatAburger, were my deacons, men full of faith and the Holy Ghost, cooking pancakes. Tables were set up where a few people, people who did

26

not especially want pancakes, but were willing to help God through this crisis, were silently nibbling at what appeared to be pancakes. I stood there as the aroma of Aunt Jemima pancakes and Log Cabin maple syrup filled the sanctuary of the Lord.

We raised 2,000 dollars that day. The following Wednesday night I told the church we still needed 2,000 dollars but we were never again going to do anything like that to raise money – at least not while I was pastor. 'If God wants this choir to go to Salt Lake City,' I said, 'he will provide in a way that will honour him and not humiliate his church.' The people agreed and we committed it to God, praying that he would supply the need according to his riches in glory.

I wondered who would donate the money; there were two or three in the church who could do it. But none of them came forward. A few days later, around six in the evening, my phone rang. It was a young woman in the church who had recently married. I knew that both she and her husband had to work to make ends meet. She said, 'Pastor, a few months before I was married I was in an automobile accident, and I received 3,000 dollars from the insurance company. I still have 2,000 dollars. All day at work I felt like I should give that to the choir trip. But I didn't want to do anything without talking to my husband. He just came in from work and before I had a chance to say anything to him, he said that he felt like God wanted us to give that 2,000 dollars to the youth choir. So that's what we want to do.'

We raised 2,000 dollars selling pancakes and 2,000 dollars by praying. When we sold the pancakes we thanked the choir members for their hard work, we thanked the deacons for giving up their Saturday to cook pancakes, we thanked WhatAburger for the silly-looking chef hats, we thanked Aunt Jemima Pancakes for selling us mix at a discount and Log Cabin Maple Syrup also – and then worried that we might have forgotten to thank someone.

When we raised 2,000 dollars by prayer, we just thanked the Lord. He got all the glory and the credit. And after all, that's what prayer is all about.

3: The Prayer God Always Answers

Some time ago a missionary told me about a letter he received from a little girl whose Sunday school class project was writing to foreign missionaries. Evidently their teacher had told them real live missionaries were very busy and might not have time to answer their letters, for the one he received said simply:

Dear Rev. Smith
We are praying for you. We are not expecting an answer.

Without realising it that little girl summed up the prayer life of many Christians: *We are praying for you. We are not expecting an answer*. The truth is, most of us aren't surprised when our prayers are unanswered – we're surprised when they are. The opposite should be true. When I flip a light switch in my house, I'm not surprised when the lights come on. When I turn on the ignition in my car I'm not surprised when the engine roars to life. And I shouldn't be surprised when God answers my prayer. God intended that our prayers be answered. While the Bible admits the fact of unanswered prayer, it never assumes it. Answered prayer should be the rule not the exception.

But prayer is one of the biggest mysteries of the Christian faith. At times, when we've had a succession of answered prayers, we feel at last we've finally learned how to pray. And then we have long stretches when God seems to have stuffed cotton in his ears and all we get is a busy signal.

No wonder the disciples said to Jesus, 'Lord, teach us to pray.' Mark it well: prayer does not come naturally or effortlessly – it must be learned. And it is good to know that we have the greatest of all teachers and that his desire to teach far surpasses our desire to learn.

In learning to pray, two problems must be dealt with: *how* to pray and *what* to pray for. Every problem we encounter in prayer revolves around these two questions – Jesus answers both in Matthew 6:1–13:

'Beware of practising your righteousness before men to be noticed by them; otherwise you have no reward with your Father who is in heaven.
'When therefore you give alms, do not sound a trumpet before you, as the hypocrites do in the synagogues and in the streets, that they may be honoured by men. Truly I say to you, they have their reward in full.
'But when you give alms, do not let your left hand know what your right hand is doing.
'That your alms may be in secret; and your Father who sees in secret will repay you.
'And when you pray, you are not to be as the hypocrites; for they love to stand and pray in the synagogues and on street corners, in order to be seen by men. Truly I say to you, they have their reward in full.
'But you, when you pray, GO INTO YOUR INNER ROOM, AND WHEN YOU HAVE SHUT YOUR DOOR, pray to your Father who is in secret, and your Father who sees in secret will repay you.
'And when you are praying, do not use meaningless repetition, as the Gentiles do, for they suppose that they will be heard for their many words.

Therefore do not be like them; for your Father knows what you need, before you ask him.
'Pray, then, in this way:

"Our Father who art in heaven,
Hallowed be thy name.

Thy kingdom come.
Thy will be done,
On earth as it is in heaven.

Give us this day our daily bread.

And forgive us our debts, as we also have forgiven our debtors.

And do not lead us into temptation, but deliver us from evil. For thine is the kingdom, and the power, and the glory, for ever.   Amen"'

(NAS)

This passage is, of course, part of the Sermon on the Mount. Here Jesus gives his disciples both the spiritual conditions and the specific content of the prayer God always answers.

Christ's purpose was not to give us merely a form prayer to be ritually recited over and over – that would contradict what he said about 'vain repetition' – but to give us an example to follow when we pray. This is a pattern, a blueprint. It covers everything in principle and contains everything that we could ask of God. Every conceivable need we will ever encounter is dealt with in the pattern prayer. When we pray, regardless of the length of our prayer, we are simply expanding the principles found here; we are adding flesh to the skeleton. This is the way to pray, says Jesus. Every prayer built according to these specifications will be answered.

Four ingredients of answered prayer emerge from these verses. But before we examine these four requirements, it will help to view the structure of the passage and see it as a whole. Here is the master teacher at work.

First, he tells us how *not* to pray, then gives the *reason* for not praying that way, and finally tells us *how* to pray. The passage falls into two easily identifiable parts.

I.   DON'T PRAY LIKE THE HYPOCRITES (verses 5,6)

1.   *The negative teaching.* Don't pray to be seen of men (verse 5a).

2.   *The reason.* You have your reward (verse 5b).

3.   *The positive teaching.* Pray in secret to the Father who is in secret (verse 6).

II. DON'T PRAY LIKE THE HEATHEN (verses 7–13).

1.   *The negative teaching.* Don't pray with meaningless repetition, thinking you will be heard because of much praying (verse 7).

2.   *The reason.* Your Father knows what you need before you ask (verse 8).

3.   *The positive teaching.* After this manner, 'pray' (verses 9–13).

Verse 6 is the cure for the wrong praying of verse 5. Verses 9–13 are cure for the wrong praying of verse 8.

Jesus warns us of the two most common dangers in prayer – praying like a hypocrite and praying like a heathen.

The hypocrite prays with the wrong motive. The heathen prays in the wrong manner.

The hypocrite perverts the purpose of prayer. The heathen misunderstands the nature of prayer.

The hypocrite prays to impress man. The heathen prays to impress God.

The hypocrite's mistake is made deliberately. The heathen's mistake is made ignorantly.

Something of the hypocrite and the heathen is in all of us. There is the temptation to use prayer to impress others and call attention to ourselves – that's the hypocrite in us. Also, we tend to rush into prayer without thought or preparation, thinking God will be persuaded by long and loud praying – that's the heathen in us. These two errors choke the life from true prayer and must be avoided. Jesus tells us how in these verses.

Now let's turn our attention to the four ingredients of the prayer God always answers.

We Must Pray With Sincerity

'And when you pray, you are not to be as the hypocrites; for they love to stand and pray in the synagogues and on street corners, in order to be seen by men. Truly I say to you, they have their reward in full' (verse 5). Prayer's first demand is sincerity. Jesus is not condemning public praying, but 'praying to be seen of men.'

Here is a sobering truth. The highest and holiest act of man is prayer; surely in the inner sanctum of the prayer closet we are safe from sin. But even here we cannot escape sin's penetrating and perverting power. Our holiest moments can become the occasion for the greatest of sins. Sin intrudes into the most sacred place and wipes its muddy feet arrogantly on the floor of the throne room.

Jesus introduced this section of the Sermon on the Mount with a warning. 'Beware of practising your righteousness before men to be noticed by them; otherwise you have no reward with your Father who is in heaven' (Matthew 6:1). Our loftiest acts are sometimes inspired by the lowest of motives. 'Vanity,' said Napoleon, 'was the cause of the revolution. Liberty was only a pretext.' It may be that in the attempt to pray we discover the truth about ourselves; perhaps in the hidden altar of prayer we meet the ultimate test of our 'interior' purity.

Our praying becomes hypocrisy when we make it a spiritual status symbol. We play the hypocrite when we use prayer to impress others. Public prayer, especially, is susceptible to this temptation. When we use prayer to draw attention to ourselves, we are in fact praying to men rather than to God, seeking their applause rather than his blessing.

This perversion of prayer can be subtle. I was away in a meeting, a thousand miles from home, eating breakfast in the hotel restaurant. When the waitress brought my plate I bowed my head and thanked God for it. Half an egg later a couple appeared at my table and asked if I was Ronald Dunn. I confessed that I was.

'When you came into the restaurant,' the man said, 'I told my wife it was you but we weren't certain.'

Then his wife said, 'I told my husband we would know it was you if you said grace over your food. We watched you, and when you bowed your head we knew it was you.'

Now when I eat alone in a restaurant I don't know if I'm praying over my food because I'm truly thankful or because someone may be watching me. When your spiritual reputation is at stake, a low motive is better than none at all.

Even our private prayer can be afflicted with this malady. Of all our spiritual activities none is as vulnerable to vain display. I think most Christians have an inferiority complex where their prayer life is concerned, and hold in awe those who have 'learned the secret' of prayer. And that makes it tempting to bid for respect by calling attention to the long hours we spend in prayer. In other words, it would be mighty hard to spend the entire night in prayer and not tell someone about it.

At no time must we be more completely sincere and totally honest than when we approach God in prayer. God welcomes us at his throne of grace when we come openly and honestly, without pretence or sham – that is, when we come with a pure motive.

Ah, and there's the rub. Nothing is as difficult to subdue as an impure motive. We are our own worst enemy. Christ's command seems so impossible we may be discouraged from praying at all. How can we achieve this degree of sincerity in prayer?

The answer lies in the next verse. 'But you, when you pray, GO INTO YOUR INNER ROOM, AND WHEN YOU HAVE SHUT THE DOOR, pray to your Father who is in secret, and your Father who sees in secret will repay you' (verse 6). This means that we must pray with secrecy.

We Must Pray With Secrecy

'The secret of religion is religion in secret.' To guard against praying to be seen of men, Jesus tells us to pray where only God can see us – in secret. By this Jesus does not mean that we are never to pray in public; the secrecy of which he speaks is more than physical, although physical secrecy is important and was practised by our Lord.

As a matter of fact, our public praying should be backed up by our private praying. If we only pray in public, we are hypocrites. Without a faithful, private prayer life our public prayers are nothing but show.

The secret praying that Jesus speaks of can be done in public. Primarily, it is a mental and spiritual secrecy. The key is the phrase, 'pray to your Father'. In public prayer we may pray to the listeners instead of God. I have been in prayer meetings where each person takes his turn praying aloud; where each prayer elicits hearty 'amens' with every phrase – until it's my turn. Have you ever noticed how quiet it suddenly gets when it's your turn to pray? And have you ever found yourself ransacking your prayer bin for one that will wring 'amens' from your fellow pray-ers?

Secret praying is 'praying to the Father'. This means that we *concentrate on his presence*. Our attention is focused on him, his will, his glory. We are more conscious of his presence than the presence of others. Having shut out the world we have shut ourselves in with him. I have heard a few people who when they prayed, even in a crowded room, prayed as though there was no one else in the universe but God and them.

Secret praying also means that we are *content with his praise*. When Jesus, referring to the praying hypocrite says, 'They have their reward,' (verse 2) he uses a word that means 'payment in full, immediate payment, nothing more to come.' And, of course, that's what the hypocrite is after – immediate reward. If he wants the praise of men, he can have it. And I think that's true of anyone: if a person sets his heart on winning the praise and approval of his contemporaries, if that is his ambition and the driving force of his life, he will probably get exactly what he wants. And anyone who wants it that badly deserves exactly what he gets. But that is all he gets. 'They have their reward,' in full and final payment.

When Jesus refers to the reward from the Father, he uses a different word, one that indicates a recompense to be paid, like interest accruing on an investment. We have a reward now in answered prayers, in the peace of God that comes through communion with him, in seeing God work in answer to our requests, in the deepening of our fellowship with him, and in a hundred more ways. But we have even more and greater rewards coming to us when we stand in his presence and receive the gifts of his praise. Nothing will satisfy the hypocrite but the praise of man; nothing will satisfy the 'secret pray-er' but the praise of God.

Imagine you are an actor or actress performing in a stage play; you are on the stage, the audience is seated before you; and when the play is done, they applaud you – you have your reward.

But when you pray before a congregation you must remember that the congregation is not the audience; you do not 'play' to them. *God is the audience*, and you 'play' to him, seeking his applause, his praise, his approval.

This kind of person will have no trouble praying sincerely in public or in private.

We Must Pray With Simplicity

In verses 7 and 8, Jesus gives us the second pitfall we must avoid in prayer – praying like the heathen: 'And when you are praying, do not use meaningless repetition, as the Gentiles do, for they suppose that they will be heard for their many words. Therefore do not be like them; for your Father knows what you need, before you ask him.'

The hypocrite's sin is praying with the wrong motive – to impress man. The heathen's sin is praying in the wrong manner – to impress God. It is not repetition that Jesus condemns, but *meaningless* repetition. The Greek word is difficult to translate into English but it carries the idea of babbling or rambling on and on in a torrent of words. 'And when you pray, do not keep on babbling like pagans,' is the New International Version's rendering.

The heathen believed their gods were impressed with the amount of time spent and words uttered in prayer. To them prayer was primarily a matter of convincing their gods that they were worthy of the blessing they were seeking. It was prayer by attrition, wearing the god down until he gives what is asked. In short, prayer was talking the god into giving them what they wanted.

It's amazing how pagan we can be in praying. Listen to yourself the next time you pray, you may find that much of your prayer is trying to talk God into seeing things your way. I admit that much of my own praying has been, at times, nothing more than an attempt to get God to believe in me, or to cooperate with me in some venture of my own making, as though I was prying open the hand of a tight-fisted God. To pray as if prayer was answered in direct proportion to the time spent on our knees, is to pray like a pagan.

Don't pray like that, Jesus tells us. Why not? 'For your Father knows what you need, before you ask him' (verse 8). The heathen prayed incorrectly because their notion of

God was incorrect; their concept of God was wrong, so their praying was wrong. We don't have that kind of God, says Jesus, so don't pray those kind of prayers.

It is God's character that determines how we pray, therefore, in prayer, the chief thing is knowing to what kind of God we are praying. Augustine prayed, 'Grant me, Lord to know which is first, to call on thee or to praise thee. And again, to know thee or to call on thee. *For who can call on thee, not knowing thee? For he that knoweth thee not may call on thee as other than thou art*' (emphasis added).

'Your Father', is how Jesus described God; and he told us to say, 'Our Father,' when we pray (verse 9). This is the first time the words, 'Our Father', are addressed to God in the Bible. You will have a difficult time finding prayers addressed to 'Our Father' in the Old Testament. This is a concept unique to the New Testament; this is how Jesus revealed God to us – 'Our Father'. And, sadly, this is a concept that seems lost to a great part of contemporary Christianity. When Jesus prayed, he said, 'Father,'* he taught us to pray, 'Our Father'; Paul's prayers were addressed to 'the God and Father of our Lord Jesus Christ'. We are instructed to pray with the simplicity of a child speaking to its father; we are to pray with the surety of a child whose father already knows its every need.

Some believe the statement that God already knows what we need implies that we need not ask. If God already knows what we need, why bother to ask? If he knows we need it and he wants us to have it, we'll get it. One popular Bible teacher said that all this business of retreating to a prayer closet and petitioning God for things is nothing but 'religious gymnastics'. The only thing wrong with that is, it's wrong.

---

* Exception: Jesus on the cross: 'My God, my God, why hast thou forsaken me?'

It is obvious that Jesus did not intend that we should interpret him that way because in the following verses (the model prayer) he tells us to pray specifically for certain things. And one of those petitions is for daily bread, which the Father surely knows we need before we ask.

These words are meant to *encourage*, not discourage, us to pray. And to pray with confidence, confidence generated by the realisation that I don't have to convince God of what I need; he is convinced before I even learn of the need.

When my son was in college, most weekends he would make the hour and a half drive home in a huge black, senile Thunderbird that I had passed down to him, which he had named 'Murphy's Law'.* When he was home I would usually inspect the beast to see if it needed any repairs. One Saturday morning he meandered nonchalantly into my study, absently looking around, and eased into a conversation about his car. He started slowly and calmly and rapidly progressed to fast and intense. He was trying to convince me that his car needed new tyres, that he didn't have the money, but the need was so urgent that maybe I could loan him the money and so on and so forth – talk about meaningless repetition. When he stopped to catch his breath I jumped in and said, 'Steve, I looked at your car this morning – I know you need new tyres.'

'You do?'

'I do.'

'When can we get them?'

His whole approach changed when he learned he didn't have to convince me of his need. 'Prayer,' said Richard Trench, 'is not overcoming God's reluctance; it is laying hold to God's willingness.'

---

* 'Murphy's Law': If anything can go wrong, it will.

39

Repetition in prayer is not always meaningless. In the two parables Jesus gave us on prayer (Luke 11:4–9; 18:1–8) the emphasis is on persistent repetition. Jesus repeated himself three times when he prayed in Gethsemane. Repetition can be the sighs of a burdened heart, a burden so intense we can't help but cry out repeatedly to God.

We Should Pray Specifically

How is this simplicity accomplished? Jesus tells us in the next verse: 'Pray, then, in this way' (verse 9). Having told us the wrong way to pray, he now shows us the right way. Simple praying is specific praying. And the specifics are laid down in the model prayer.

As I mentioned earlier, Jesus intended the prayer to be more than a formal benediction. It is good and right that we should use it in our worship, both in private and in public. But that is not its paramount purpose. It is first and foremost a pattern to guide us in our praying.

Two facts deserve notice: one, prayer is an *act*. While we should live in an attitude of prayer, prayer is more than an attitude. It is not merely, as one put it, living in the awareness that all things are ours in Christ. For Christ, prayer was an act with an beginning and an ending: 'When Jesus *ceased* praying' (Luke 11:1, emphasis added); 'When you *pray, say,*' (Luke 11:2, emphasis added).

Two, prayer is *asking*. Prayer is petition, not praise. Our private worship should, of course, include praise, and during times of prayer we should praise God, but prayer and praise are not the same thing. Of the various biblical words used to denote prayer the vast majority are, almost without exception, unashamedly words of petition.

I labour this point because the church seems to have rediscovered praise – and there is tremendous emphasis on it in both teaching and singing. But the momentum created by this emphasis has caused some to overshoot the point of balance. Not long ago a fellow conference speaker, in a message on praise, stated that as we mature in Christ, praise will replace petition – there will be less asking and more praising. He went so far as to suggest that if we are still at the 'petition level' of prayer, we are carnal. I was barely able to resist the urge to leap up and say, 'If that is so then Jesus was carnal,' because his prayers were almost totally prayers of petition – petitions for himself. The prayers of Paul were petitionary. Both Christ and Paul admonished us to ask and keep on asking.

The model prayer is one-hundred per cent petition. Even the phrase, 'Hallowed be thy name', is petition, not praise. Jesus was not saying, 'When you pray, the first thing you should do is hallow the name of the Father.' He said, 'When you pray, say, "Thy name be hallowed".' That is a petition, praying that God's name will be hallowed and revered.

The prayer is made up of six petitions, imperatives in the form of commands. In each instance we are asking God to do something specific. The prayer is in two parts, with three petitions in each part. The full exposition of the prayer demands a volume of its own; here we can only mention the main points.

The first part of the prayer concerns *The Glory of the Father* (verses 9,10).

The prayer God always answers gives priority to the glory of the Father, putting his interests before our own. This implies an emptying of self and an occupation with the things of God. Only after we have thus forgotten ourselves can we think of ourselves.

1. We are to pray that the name of God will be revered. 'Hallowed be thy name.'

2. We are to pray that the rule of God will be established. 'Thy kingdom come.'

3. We are to pray that the will of God will be done. 'Thy will be done.'

The second part of the prayer concerns *The Good of the Family*, physically and spiritually.

1. We are to pray for daily provision. 'Give us this day our daily bread.'

2. We are to pray for daily pardon. 'Forgive us our debts.'

3. We are to pray for daily protection. 'Do not lead us into temptation, but deliver us from evil.'

At the beginning of the model prayer is a phrase that casts its shadow over the entire prayer, setting the stage for its petitions and forming the foundation of all true prayer – 'Our Father'. These two words sum up the whole prayer.

Our. It is so obvious we often miss it. *Our* Father. *Our* daily bread. *Our* debts. Lead *us*. Deliver *us*. This is a *family* prayer. No child of God ever prays alone. In a sense, when one child prays, the entire family prays. Here is a hint of what Jesus would mean later when he would pray for his followers, 'that they may all be one; even as thou, Father, art in me, and I in thee . . . .' (John 17:21).

Our. This is intercession – unselfish intercession. The family member prays, not only for himself, but for every member of the family. What he seeks for himself, he seeks for the whole family. As a member of the family of God, as a constituent of its oneness, I have no right to ask something for myself that I wouldn't want every member to have. Whatever prayer finally is, it is not a means whereby I can forge ahead of others, possess more than others, occupy a more favoured position with the Father, enable my church to grow larger and wealthier than the church across the street.

Father is the other word – '*Our Father*'. Here is the requirement of all prayer. Prayer is a family matter and only those who can say, 'Our Father', can truly pray.

Here is our right to pray. We are not beggars cowering at the back door pleading for a handout: we are children seated at the Father's table. J. D. Jones tells the story of a Roman emperor who was entering Rome in triumph after a victorious battle. As the magnificent procession moved down the street, a small child suddenly darted through the fence of soldiers lining the street, and headed for the opulent carriage that bore the emperor. One of the soldiers grabbed him, saying, 'That is the emperor!'

The child broke loose and, racing for the carriage, cried back, '*Your* emperor, *My* father!'

What right have we to imagine God would suffer the likes of us in his throne room, and listen to our pitiful requests?

When you pray, say, '*Our Father*'.

4: A Lesson in Intercession

The most frightening sound in the world is a telephone ringing in the middle of the night.

It never happens without reminding me of the Psalmist's words, 'He will not be afraid of evil tidings; his heart is steadfast, trusting in the Lord' (Psalm 112:7).

My phone was ringing at 4.00 am. Only a couple of hours before I had collapsed into bed after a long trip from New Mexico and I knew this phone call meant another seven or eight hours on the road, with no rest at the end. It was my brother telling me that our mother had died – of cancer, after fifty days in the hospital.

We threw some clothes into a couple of suitcases, dragged the kids out of bed and beat the sun to the highway by an hour. Mercifully, it was a trouble-free trip and we arrived in fair condition.

That was August. In September, sitting in a friend's house in Colorado, I mentioned Mom's death. My friend stood suddenly and said, 'What day was that?'

I told her the date as she disappeared into another room; in a moment she was back, flipping through the pages of a notebook.

'Here it is,' she said. She read the date and the entry. It was a prayer diary, and on that August Sunday morning, long before sunrise, she awoke with a burden to pray for my family and me, an unrelenting burden that stayed with her most of the day.

I couldn't help but think of what Jesus said to Peter in the upper room the night he was betrayed. Having told

Peter that Satan was going to sift him as wheat, he said, 'But I have prayed for you, that your faith should not fail; and when you have returned to me, strengthen your brethren' (Luke 22:32).

I'm glad Jesus didn't say, 'If you return to me,' as though the outcome was uncertain. He said, 'When you have returned to me . . . .'

The intercession of Christ prevented the failure of Peter's faith (his love failed and his courage failed, but not his faith) and opened the way for his recovery.

We are never more like Christ than when we are praying for others. Intercession is laying down our life for our friend; it is bearing one another's burden; it is sharing in the sufferings of Christ. The work of redemption, as I've already said, is the work of intercession. Jesus is interceding, the Holy Spirit is interceding, and we are to intercede. Paul closes his passage on spiritual warfare (Ephesians 6:10–17) with a plea for intercessory prayer: 'Praying always with all prayer and supplication in the Spirit, being watchful to this end with all perseverance and supplication *for all the saints* – and for me, that utterance may be given to me, that I may open my mouth boldly to make known the mystery of the gospel' (Ephesians 6:18,19 emphasis added).

God has made us a royal priesthood with the privilege and the responsibility to pray for one another, which ought to drive us to ask, as did the disciples, 'Lord, teach us to pray' (Luke 11:1).

He did. And he will teach us also.

Jesus answered the disciples' request, first with the model prayer, then with the parable of the friend at midnight. The parable is powerful illustration of intercession, involving three parties. Intercession is a triangle of prayer: one person going to another person to get bread for a third person.

And he said to them, 'Which of you shall have a friend, and go to him at midnight and say to him, "Friend, lend me three loaves;

"For a friend of mine has come to me on his journey, and I have nothing to set before him";

'And he will answer from within and say, "Do not trouble me; the door is now shut, and my children are with me in bed; I cannot rise and give to you"?

'I say to you, though he will not rise and give to him because he is his friend, yet because of his persistence he will rise and give him as many as he needs' (Luke 11:5–8).

Intercession is Daring Praying

Daring, bold, audacious – these are the only adjectives that rightly describe intercessory praying.

The situation in the story called for boldness. The hour was inconvenient – it was midnight. The circumstances were inconvenient – 'my children are in bed with me'. Williams translates: 'my children are packed about me in bed'. It was common in those days for whole families to sleep together, not only for warmth, but also because of a lack of space. The typical one room dwelling would contain one large mat on which the entire family slept – usually including a few farm animals.

But this doesn't dissuade the midnight caller. He bangs on the door and keeps banging until lights come on in the neighbours' houses and dogs start barking.

Daring, boldness – all the intercessors of the Bible had this. Two of those intercessors, Abraham and Moses, we will look at again in this book.

Listen to Abraham as he intercedes for godless Sodom: 'Would you also destroy the righteous with the wicked? Far be it from you to do such a thing as this . . . Shall not the Judge of all the earth do right?' (Genesis 18:23–25). Every time I read that I have an urge to remind Abraham who he's talking to. That's daring praying.

Moses was another bold intercessor. A drama is unfolding in Exodus 32. While Moses has been with God on the mountain, the people have gone wild. They have forgotten the Lord who saved them and have bowed down to worship a god made with their own hands, a golden calf.

When the people 'rose up to play', God rose up to judge: 'And the Lord said to Moses, "Go, get down! For your people whom you brought out of the land of Egypt have corrupted themselves."' His patience was exhausted, he was through with them, finished, end of story. 'I have seen this people, and indeed it is a stiff-necked people! Now, therefore, let me alone, that my wrath may burn hot against them and I may consume them' (Exodus 32:7,10).

But Moses intercedes for them: 'Turn from your fierce wrath, and relent from this harm to your people' (verse 12). Notice God called them Moses' people, but Moses calls them God's people.

In his prayer Moses makes two bold statements. First, he tells God that destroying his own people will ruin his reputation; the Egyptians will mock and say that God delivered them from Egypt so he could kill them in the mountains (verse 12).

Second, if God did this he would be breaking his promise and violating his own word: 'Remember Abraham, Isaac, and Israel, your servants, to whom you swore by your own self' that they would inherit the land for ever (verse 13).

The result? 'So the Lord relented from the harm which he said he would do to his people' (verse 14). Think of it – one man wielding the weapon of intercession saved an entire nation.

Intercession is Stubborn Praying

The most critical part of the story in Luke 11 is verse 8 where Jesus says, 'I say to you, though he will not rise and give to him because he is his friend, yet because of his persistence he will rise and give him as many as he needs.'

The word translated 'friend' is a strong one and indicates more than a casual or ordinary acquaintance. It is a term of endearment, 'to love as a brother'. This is an impossible thing – that you would turn away from your door, whatever the hour, a man you loved like a brother. No one would do that. But this man does. What we have here are two very stubborn men: one man determined to get bread, the other just as determined not to give it. If this man whose heart is as shut as his door won't give in to brotherly love, what will he give in to? If friendship can't make him open his door, what can?

Importunity. That's the old King James word for persistence. 'Because of his *persistence* he will rise and give him as many as he needs.' But the word is stronger than persistence. It is a lack of shame, shamelessness. Most of us would be embarrassed if we created such a commotion and our best friend told us to go away. I would be so humiliated I wouldn't show my face around there for months. But not this fellow; he doesn't even have the capacity to be embarrassed. He was born without a nerve of shame, he never feels it. Therefore, he is persistent. But he is stubbornly, shamelessly persistent. He has gall.

Evidently Jesus considered this shameless stubbornness an advantage in praying because he emphasised it again in the parable of the widow and the unjust judge (Luke 18:1–8). The judge, with no fear of God and no regard for man, refused to aid a widow who came to him seeking justice. This is an unbelievable scenario. How could anyone refuse to help a widow? That's the point.

But although there was no pity in the judge, there was importunity in the widow. The judge said to himself, 'Though I do not fear God nor regard man, yet because this widow troubles me I will avenge her, lest by her continual coming she wearies me' (verses 4,5). *Yet* is emphasised in the Greek text; it is the critical point in this story. It is the widow's 'continual coming' that persuades the judge, not a change of heart on his part.

Incidentally, 'weary' is a translation of a word that means to hit someone in the eye, to give someone a black eye. This is a tough widow – the judge was afraid she would beat him black and blue.

Now listen to Jesus' application of the story: 'Then the Lord said, "Hear what the unjust judge said." And shall God not avenge his own elect who cry out day and night to him, though he bears long with them? I tell you that he will . . . .' (verses 6–8). If an unjust judge will surrender to the persistent pleading of a widow, how much more will God honour the persistence of his own people?

Do you recall the Old Testament story about Jacob wrestling with an angel (Genesis 32:24–32)? Something about that has always bothered me. This is an angel that Jacob is fighting, an angel who wants to get away, but Jacob won't let him. 'Let me go, for the day breaks,' the angel says. And Jacob says, 'I will not let you go unless you bless me!' (verse 26). Now here's what bothers me – have you ever seen an angel that couldn't break away from a mere human if he really wanted to? Do you believe that Jacob was so strong he could pin down an angel? *That fight was fixed.* I believe that while the angel was saying, 'Let me go,' he was whispering under his breath, 'But I hope you don't. Hang on a little longer and you'll get the blessing.'

I wonder how many times we have stopped short of the blessing? Would Sodom have been saved if Abraham had not stopped at ten? Could our church, our city, our country see a spiritual awakening if we pray like Jacob: 'I will not let you go until you bless me!'?

Intercession is Sacrificial Praying

Intercession is a ministry of sacrifice. There can be no true intercession outside the fellowship of Christ's sufferings.

The intercessor in our story was called upon to make several sacrifices. He forfeited his sleep and rest; he placed his friendship on the line, risking it to feed a stranger. The whole affair was an inconvenience to him. But the key sacrifice was this: he identified himself with the traveller and the traveller's need.

This man was not hungry, he didn't need bread – it was his guest who was hungry. Let him do his own begging, then. If he wants it badly enough, let him do it. But the host acted as though he was the hungry one. He took his guest's place, and that is the essence of intercession.

To intercede we identify ourselves with the needs of others. The hurt ones listen for a cry like their own, a cry that tells them they are not alone. That cry is our prayer. The cry cost them plenty and our affirming cry will cost us . . . something.

We can follow the tracks of Jesus here. When God set out to redeem mankind he identified himself with man by becoming a man and walking where man walked. That is what the incarnation is all about. God did not come to us as an invisible, inaccessible, unapproachable, unknowable God – he came to us as a man, with man's feelings, man's temptations and man's limitations – he came so close that John said he *handled with his own hands* the very word of Life (1 John 1:1; 'handled' is used of a blind man's groping, emphasising the realness of the handling).

Jesus' baptism was an act of indentification with sinners. The baptism of John was a baptism of confession and repentance of sin. That's why none of the Pharisees lined up to be baptised by John – that would have been an admission of sin. When Jesus asked John to baptise him, John protested: 'I have need to be baptised by you, and are you coming to me?' (Matthew 3:14). There was no reason to baptise Jesus – he had no sin.

But there was a reason: it was to be clear from the beginning of his ministry that Jesus had come to identify himself with sinners and John's baptism (a baptism of repentance) was a part of that declaration.

Jesus is named for every need of man: to the hungry he is the Bread of life; to the thirsty, he is the Fountain of Living Waters; to the sick, he is the Balm of Gilead; to the dying, he is the Resurrection and the Life; to the lonely, the Friend that sticks closer than a brother; and to the outcast, he is the Friend of Sinners. The crescendo of our Lord's indentification with man was reached at the cross – there he was numbered with the transgressors (Isaiah 53:12).

Again, Moses instructs us. He shows how identification is the prelude to intercession. If we look once more at Moses' prayer in Exodus 32:32, we hear him say to God, 'Yet now, if you will forgive their sin – but if not, I pray, blot me out of your book which you have written.' While there is much we do not understand in Moses' request, one thing is clear: Moses identified himself with his people.

Moving to the New Testament, Paul gives us a glimpse into the mystery of identification in Romans 9:1–3. 'I tell the truth in Christ, I am not lying, my conscience also bearing me witness in the Holy Spirit, that I have great sorrow and continual grief in my heart. *For I could wish that I myself were accursed of Christ for my brethren, my kinsmen according to the flesh*' (emphasis added). Theologians have spun their wheels in these verses for years, but again, whatever else Paul may have meant by these words, one thing is clear: his burden for his brethren was so great and his sorrow so overwhelming, he was willing to identify himself with them. And that is intercession. No wonder then that in the first verse of the next chapter we hear Paul say, 'Brethren, my heart's desire and prayer to God for Israel is that they may be saved.'

The pre-eminent requirement for intercession is the willingness to identify ourself with the one in need, the readiness to take to ourself his burden. It is, in the purest sense, 'laying down our lives for the brethren'.

Jesus pointed the way to a spiritual harvest in these words: 'Most assuredly, I say to you, unless a grain of wheat falls into the ground and dies, it remains alone; but if it dies, it produces much grain' (John 12:24). The phrase, 'it remains alone', indicts us all. There is little room for argument here – if our life does not bring forth fruit, we have not yet learned to die.

Paul reinforces this in 2 Corinthians. Describing his life, he said that he was 'always carrying about in the body the dying of the Lord Jesus, that the life of Jesus also may be manifested in our body.

'For we who live are always delivered to death for Jesus' sake, that the life of Jesus also may be manifested in our mortal flesh.

'*So then death is working in us, but life in you*' (2 Corinthians 4:10–12 emphasis added). Let these words sink in. Here is the law of spiritual harvest: '*death is working in us, but life in you.*'

For Jesus, the victory was won in the garden where he prayed, 'Your will be done.' When he left Gethsemane the issue of the cross was finally and for ever settled. And every intercessor has his own Garden of Gethsemane where the real battle is waged. In intercession the battle is won or lost at the point of our willingness to enter into Christ's suffering and identify ourselves with others to the point of sacrifice.

Let's pause here and measure our progress. Here, then, is the pattern of intercession:

Identifying ourselves with the needs of others;

   Sacrificing to meet those needs;

      Authority to obtain those needs.

This pattern is seen in the friend at midnight. He *identified* himself with the need of his guest, acting as if he were the hungry one. He *sacrificed* to meet that need, giving up physical comfort and convenience to go out into the night seeking bread. And from his identification and sacrifice came *authority* to obtain all he needed from his reluctant friend.

Moses *identified* himself with his people: '. . . but if not, I pray, blot me out of your book which you have written.' He *sacrificed* for them, praying and fasting forty days on the mountain. And he certainly gained *authority* with God in prayer, for though God did chasten them with plagues, he did not consume his people or cast them away.

Jesus *identified* himself with man by taking on the form of a servant. He *sacrificed* himself for man by taking our sins in his own body on the tree. And with all *authority* in heaven and earth, he loosed man from his sins, stripped Satan of his armour, tore the sting out of death and flung open wide the gates of glory.

We follow in their train. The servant is not above his master. Make no mistake about it: prevailing intercession will cost us – sleepless nights, unseen tears, the sacrifice of personal desire and convenience, and whatever else is necessary to fill up that which is lacking in the sufferings of Christ (Colossians 1:24). 'When Zion travailed, she brought forth her children.' Nature itself teaches us there can be no life without travail.

Gaining the Position

Which brings us to the real key to effective intercession. Intercession is more than prayer. Prayer is a form and expression of intercession, but it alone is not intercession. Intercession is not petition. Intercession is *position*. It is not something we do – it is something we are. It is not an exercise we engage in at certain times of the day, it is a life that we live.

In Ezekiel 22 verse 30, God sought for a man from among them to make a wall, 'to stand in the gap before him . . .' Here God does not say that he is looking necessarily for someone to pray – he is seeking a man who will assume a certain position and live a certain life.

Jeremiah describes a similar search. 'Run to and fro through the streets of Jerusalem; see now and know; and seek in her open places if you can find a man, if there is anyone who executes judgment, who seeks the truth, and I will pardon her' (Jeremiah 5:1).

God is looking for a man who will execute justice and speak the truth. He doesn't say he wants a man who can pray, although that would certainly play a part; he is looking primarily for someone who will live a certain kind of life, who will assume a particular position.

Intercession is gaining a certain position and praying from that position. Intercession is 'positional praying'.

In the case of Christ, Isaiah said he 'made intercession for the transgressor' Isaiah 53:12). Isaiah does not mean only that Jesus prayed for transgressors, he lived for them and died for them. His entire life, his ministry, his humiliation, his agony – all of it was intercession. The Bible says he is now seated at the right hand of God – to do what? To make intercession for us. He assumed a position and is now praying from that position.

An Illustration

Throughout my ministry I have been intrigued by a certain fact. I have seen scores of Christian wives with unsaved husbands. And often they were among the most faithful workers in the church. But I can count on one hand the number of Christian husbands in my churches whose wives were unsaved. A faithful Christian wife whose husband is lost is routine. On the other hand, in my experience, a Christian husband with an unsaved wife is rare.

Perhaps that's part of the reason for the words in 1 Peter 3: apostolic advice to Christian wives on winning their lost husbands. But nothing similar to husbands with unsaved wives. Here is Peter's counsel to wives who want to win their husbands:

'Wives, in the same way be submissive to your husbands so that, if any of them do not believe the word, they may be won over without talk by the behaviour of their wives, when they see the purity and reverence of your lives' (1 Peter 3:1,2 NIV).

A wife may win her lost husband to Christ without saying a word to him about it. Let's face it, some individuals can be reached by only one person and in only one way. Here it is the wife, and it is by her life that her husband is saved, not by being dragged to church or hounded by the pastor or preached to by the wife, but as he sees ('watches attentively' is the meaning) the purity and reverence of her life. 'Your beauty,' Peter continues, 'should not come from outward adornment, such as braided hair and the wearing of gold jewellery and fine clothes (note: Peter is not saying the wife should not braid her hair and wear jewellery or fine clothes. There's nothing wrong with those things, but they will not win him to Christ). Instead, it should be that of your inner self, the unfading beauty of a gentle and quiet spirit, which is of great worth in God's sight' (verses 3,4 NIV).

The wife wins her husband, not by petition only, but by *position* – the position of submissiveness, purity and reverence and the unfading beauty of a gentle and quiet spirit. And when she gains this position, her entire life becomes an act of intercession. When she cooks his favourite dish and listens to a boring story about the fish that got away, or endures with grace the post-season football games, she is interceding. When, with a Christ-like spirit she accepts his careless treatment of her, she is interceding. Every beat of her heart is intercession, every drop of blood that flows through her veins is a petition. Every tear that falls from her eyes because of his indifference is a prayer lifted to God.

55

If, then, intercession is a position we live in and pray from, the question is: how is that position gained? As always, Christ is our teacher and example. It is a position gained by sacrificial submissiveness; it requires a servant attitude, the attitude of Christ Paul describes in the second chapter of Philippians.

Here, then, is the making of an intercessor: 'Let nothing be done through selfish ambition or conceit, but in lowliness of mind let each esteem others better than himself.

'Let each of you look out not only for his own interests, but also for the interests of others.

'Let this mind be in you which was also in Christ Jesus' who took upon himself the form of a servant and humbled himself to the point of death (Philippians 2:3–8).

The 'mind of Christ' took centre stage the night the Lord ate his last supper with the disciples in the upper room (John 13). Jesus startled them when he took off his outer garment, girded himself with a towel and proceeded to wash the feet of the twelve – including the feet of Judas. Peter was horrified. Even he, a poor fisherman, would not be expected to wash the feet of another. That was given to the lowest servant in the household. That was a task for the Gentile-dog servants. He said, 'Lord, you can't wash my feet!'

But for all his protesting, even after Jesus said it was an act of humbling service they should do for one another, Peter never volunteered to wash feet. He did not say, 'Lord, give me the towel and water. I'll wash your feet.' No, there was no such word from Peter or from any of the others. And when they withdrew from the room that night only one left with unwashed feet, the one who came not to be ministered to, but to minister and to offer his life as a ransom.

In the making of the great intercessor, Paul leads us from his *humiliation* and *submission* to his *identification*:

he 'made himself of no reputation, taking the form of a servant, and coming in the likeness of men' (verse 7). Next came his *crucifixion*: 'And being found in appearance as a man, he humbled himself and became obedient to the point of death, even the death of the cross' (verse 8).

Now see the end of all this: his *exaltation*: 'Therefore God also has highly exalted him and given him the name which is above every name . . .' (verse 9).

Here is the path to intercession:

Humiliation and Submission;

Identification and Crucifixion;

Exaltation and Intercession.

As the intercessor for transgressors, Christ was the answer to his own prayer. From the cross, Jesus prayed for his crucifiers, 'Father, forgive them for they know not what they do.' Yet Jesus' death was the answer to his own prayer. The only basis upon which the Father could forgive them was that very act of crucifixion, for without the shedding of blood there is no remission.

Only as death works in us will life work in those we pray for. That is the law of the spiritual harvest (2 Corinthians 4:11,12). And I believe when we, in order to stand in the gap for another, take to ourselves voluntary death to advantage and ambition, to consideration, comfort and convenience, we have the right to expect a spiritual harvest.

Are we ready to assume that position?

Intercession is Desperate Praying

Only desperate men and women, propelled by a sense of urgency, truly intercede. Those who are 'at ease in Zion' will never man the ramparts of intercession to repel the enemy. The indifferent will not be found among the watchmen set upon the walls who 'never hold their peace day or night'. Battles are not won by the nonchalant. And even if one of these should try to intercede they will soon be sidetracked into more 'practical' endeavours. What praying they might do will be neutralised by their half-heartedness.

A cry of desperation sounds throughout this parable. It would have been easy to convince a casual host to wait for a more practical hour to go banging on his neighbour's door. Unconcern always finds an excuse, deep concern always finds a way. Only desperate people take desperate actions and prevail.

Vance Havner used to say, 'The problem is, the situation is desperate but we're not!'

But we should be. Our inescapable responsibility should make us desperate. A friend of mine has come to me on his journey. He has come *to me*. Not to my neighbour, not to my pastor, but to me. He is my responsibility. It was an unwritten law that if a traveller stopped at your door, seeking food and refuge, you supplied his needs. Failure to do so was a serious breach of social obligation and jeopardised the life of the traveller.

And there are people, who in their journey, have come to us. They live next door, they sit behind us at school, they work in the same office with us, and we are the only Christians they meet. They are our inescapable responsibility.

There is a fascinating word the New Testament often uses when talking of the first Christians. It's the word 'scattered', somtimes translated, 'dispersed'. Luke uses this word to depict the Christians' reaction to persecution in Acts 8:1,4: '. . . and they were all scattered throughout the regions of Judea and Samaria . . . . Therefore those who were scattered went everywhere preaching the word.'

In Acts 11:19 the word occurs again: 'Now those who were scattered after the persecution that arose over Stephen travelled as far as Phoenicia, Cyprus and Antioch.'

Peter uses the same word in 1 Peter 1:1. 'Peter, an apostle of Jesus Christ, to the pilgrims of the *Dispersion* (scattering) in Pontus, Galatia, Cappadocia, Asia and Bithynia' (emphasis added). The Jewish 'diaspora' came about through deportation and other means, some voluntary, some not, to move them to a foreign land. Peter uses the word for believers who are scattered throughout the world and yet still have hope of one day being gathered back to the land.

And James uses the word in his epistle. 'James, a servant of God and of the Lord Jesus Christ, to the twelve tribes which are scattered abroad' (James 1:1).

What makes this word so interesting, of course, is its meaning: 'to sow seed throughout, the scattering abroad of seed by the sower'. Because of persecution, Christians were scattered everywhere. But see what God was doing – he was sowing seed throughout the world so there could be a great harvest of souls. The believers of the twelve tribes of the Dispersion were seed sown by God in different fields.

Do you think you just chanced into that particular house on that particular street? Could it be that God wanted a harvest there and you are the seed he planted? Think about it.

You may say your company transferred you to this area and that's the only reason you are here. Perhaps it is more than that. Perhaps God is sowing seed in that community, and your company is the instrument he used to do the sowing, just as he used persecution to plant the early Christians in new lands.

Maybe God planted you where you are because he knew that a friend in his journey would pass your way, and maybe God wants you to identify with his need and in Jesus' name meet that need. He is your inescapable responsibility.

Our inadequate resources should also make us desperate. Listen to the plaintive words of the host, 'And I have nothing to set before him.' His words echo our own desperation in the face of the life-and-death responsibilities God has placed within our borders.

'Lord, my neighbour is lost and dying of cancer – and I have nothing to set before him.'

'Lord, I have a teenage daughter facing severe temptation – and I have nothing to set before her.'

'Lord, the man I work with, his home is breaking up – and I have nothing to set before him.'

Who is sufficient for these things? No one. And that should drive us to the throne of grace 'that we may obtain mercy and find grace to help in time of need' (Hebrews 4:16). If the church does not learn to knock boldly at the Father's door her magnificent sanctuaries will become empty breadboxes, and starving travellers, finding no bread in her doors, will turn away from the choreographed worship with empty stomachs and aching bellies.

If a man gets hungry enough he'll eat bread from a rubbish bin. And you can be sure that if he walks away from the church empty-handed, the devil will be waiting for him with plenty of rubbish bin bread.

I've never forgotten the native evangelist from Khartoum, Sudan who visited our church one Sunday morning. Before the worship service we knelt in my study and he prayed, 'Father, if you don't bless the pastor today, the people will go away hungry'. I can still hear the urgency in his voice.

Jehoshaphat was a desperate man. His story is told in 2 Chronicles. For twenty-five years he reigned as king of Judah and 'his heart took delight in the ways of the Lord' (17:6). Building on the godly foundation laid by his father, Asa, this reformer-king destroyed the wooden images and the places of pagan worship in Judah. The Bible says that from Beersheba to the mountains of Ephraim, he brought the people 'back to the Lord God of their fathers' (19:4).

Everything was going great – until the day news came that the Moabites and the Ammonites were moving against Judah. As a matter of fact, they were camping on the banks of the Dead Sea, already within striking distance of Jerusalem (don't you find interesting that the enemy strikes in the midst of Judah's spiritual revival?).

'And Jehoshaphat feared, and set himself to seek the Lord, and proclaimed a fast throughout all Judah' (20:3). The people came from all over Judah and gathered in Jerusalem to seek the Lord. Then Jehoshaphat stood in the congregation of Judah and Jerusalem in the house of the Lord and threw himself upon God. Listen to his prayer: 'O our God, will you not judge them? For we have no power against this great multitude that is coming against us; nor do we know what to do, but our eyes are upon you' (20:12).

Jehoshaphat is in dire straits – Judah has no power against this bunch, and even if they did, they wouldn't know what to do with it. 'Nor do we know what to do.' This is the king talking; if anyone ought to know what to do, it is him. What hope is there if the king himself is helpless?

All of us are familiar with the nauseating sense of helplessness that sweeps over us when we have exercised all our options and have exhausted all our funds. 'There come moments in every life when the false security in which shallow souls wrap themselves ignobly is broken up, and then often a paroxysm of terror or misery grips a man . . . and his despair is as unreasonable as his security.'[1]

'We do not know what to do' – but that's not the end of the story. Helplessness isn't the final word. *But* is the final word: 'but our eyes are upon you.' We look at the enemy and we see our powerlessness, we look at our cleverness and we see our ignorance, but the last look is toward God. God meets us at the point of desperation.

Which leads to the final point in our parable: God's inevitable reward. 'He will rise and give him as many as

61

he needs' (v 8). Did he get three loaves? I don't know. But he got as many as he needed. No one goes away from the Father empty-handed. The promise of Christ is , 'If you then, being evil, know how to give good gifts to your children, how much more will your Father who is in heaven give good things to those who ask him?' (Matthew 7:11).

Remember Jehoshaphat. As he sought God's help, the Spirit of the Lord came upon one of the Levitical singers, who said, 'Thus says the Lord to you: "Do not be afraid or dismayed because of this great multitude, for the battle is not yours, but God's"' (20:15). That was a welcome piece of news. Does that sound familiar? It should. That's what David said to Goliath. 'This day the Lord will deliver you into my hand . . . and all this assembly shall know that the Lord does not save with sword and spear; *for the battle is the Lord's,* and he will give you into our hands' (1 Samuel 17:46,47 emphasis added).

The Levite went on to say to Jehoshaphat and the congregation, 'You will not need to fight in this battle. Position yourselves, stand still and see the salvation of the Lord' (20:17). And a strange battle it was. The Marine band and chorus went out first, ahead of the soldiers, saying, 'Praise the Lord, for his mercy endures for ever.' The singers before the soldiers – 'and when they began to sing and to praise, the Lord set ambushes against the people of Ammon, Moab, and Mount Seir, who had come against Judah; and they were defeated' (vv 21,22).

The victory was won in the place of prayer. Prayer decided the outcome before Judah ever set foot on the battlefield.

And the reward? It took them three days to pick up the spoils of victory. 'When Jehoshaphat and his people came to take away the spoil, they found among them an abundance of valuables on the dead bodies, and precious jewellerry, which they stripped off themselves, more than they could carry away; and they were there three days gathering the spoil because there was so much' (v 25).

We, like Jehoshaphat and his people, enter the place of intercession with our *much need* and come away with his *much more*.

There is only one place to get bread – from the Father. And there is only one way to get it – by asking.

5: Praying For Others

One summer I took my family to the south coast of Texas, thinking that the gentle rhythm of the waves sliding back and forth across the Gulf coast beaches might wash a little calm into our souls.

It had not been a good year and it was only half over. A few days before we left, our youngest son added variety to the situation by breaking his leg. He now wore a cast from his hip to his toes. The x-rays showed not only the break but some tumour-like growths on the bone. Too soon yet to know what they were. I used my imagination.

So there we were, soaking up sun and surf at in-season rates. And every morning when I woke up, there *he* was, waiting for me beside the bed – the waves had not carried away my gloomy companion – depression. I couldn't shake him. We went everywhere together, me and my shadow.

Until Thursday morning. I woke up and he wasn't there. All day long I expected him to leap out from some dark alley, but there wasn't a sign of him. I relaxed from the inside out. Not a single thing had changed, but everything was different.

Back home a few days later, I went to my office to pick up the mail that had piled up while I was away. One of the letters bore a hotel letterhead but I recognised the handwriting; it was from a friend who knew everything about my situation. Next to the date was the time the letter had been written: 3.00 am.

Dear Ron

I have prayed for you today and am about to pray again that God will make this time through which you are passing a new door open to the mystery of truth. God must love you so much to watch you pass through this trying time . . . .

So, no sermons at this point. I am going to say the thing that means the most to me at this moment with reference to you. I have no friend on the face of the earth whose friendship I treasure more than yours. I have asked God to put on my heart as much burden as he can to lighten yours. I want to bear it with you. That does not require conversation or correspondence. But in the spiritual realm where those transactions are tendered I have bartered for your burden . . .

I was not surprised to see that the date on the letter was the Thursday I awoke without my sepulchral companion waiting for me.

Is this what Paul had in mind when he told us to bear one another's burdens? Is this what Martin Luther meant when, feeling unusually strong and happy, he would say, 'I feel as if I were being prayed for'? This is surely what T. DeWitt Talmadge had in mind when he said, 'The mightiest thing you can do for a man is to pray for him.'

The Triangle of Intercession

Prayer was certainly the 'mightiest thing' the early church did for Peter. Around the time that Paul and Barnabas were on their way to Jerusalem with aid from the church at Antioch, Herod the king began to terrorise the young church (Acts 12:1). First, he killed James, the brother of John. That delighted the Jews so much he decided to kill Peter also. He seized Peter and threw him in jail with 16 men set to guard him. In the morning

Peter would follow James down the path to martyrdom. But . . .

'Peter was therefore kept in prison, *but* constant prayer was offered to God for him by the church' (Acts 12:5 emphasis added). See the contrast: Peter was kept in prison – but – constant prayer was made by the church to God for him. Peter imprisoned and facing death was not the last word on the matter; the last word was, and still can be, 'prayer was offered to God for him by the church'.

Do you find it interesting, as I do, that the martyrdom of James merits only eleven words (that's in the New King James Version. Only seven words in the Greek text)? But Peter's episode requires seventeen verses. The story is told in a deliberate manner to highlight the confrontation taking place. It is the conflict between the world and the church, a conflict that persists to this day. It is political power pitted against prayer power.

Luke writes the story like a novelist. The details are delicious. Herod delivered Peter to four four-man squads, sixteen guards; Peter was rescued on the very night Herod intended to bring him out for execution; Peter slept between two guards, bound by two chains; guards were at the door which was an iron gate; an angel stood by Peter, kicked him in the side to wake him up, told him to get up, gird himself, tie on his sandals, put on his garment and said, 'Follow me.'

They went past the first guard post, the second guard post, then came to the iron gate of the city, 'which opened to them of its own accord' (verse 10), literally, 'automatically'. Luke is enjoying himself. He is revelling in the triumph of the praying church.

Is there a better picture of the triangle of intercession than the praying of this young church? Constant prayer (1) to God (2) for him and (3) by the church.

This young church knew that it was, and always would be, as was its founder, in deadly conflict with the world.

It also knew that its power to confront and conquer that conflict lay in prayer. What it did not know was *how much* power it had. But it was about to find out.

Once safely outside the prison, the angel left Peter. When he came to himself and realised he wasn't dreaming and that he had really been delivered by the angel of the Lord, he headed straight for the house of Mary where he knew his fellow believers would be gathered.

When he knocked on the door, a girl named Rhoda went to answer. 'When she recognised Peter's voice, because of her gladness she did not open the gate, but ran in and announced that Peter stood before the gate' (verse 14). Isn't that tremendous? God had answered their prayers – Peter was standing at the door! While they were knocking at heaven's door with the request, God was knocking at their door with the answer.

And what did they say when they heard the news? Are you ready for this? They said, 'You're crazy!'

'But they said to her, "You are beside yourself!" Yet she kept insisting that it was so. So they said, "It is his angel."

Now Peter continued knocking; and when they opened the door and saw him, they were astonished' (verses 15,16).

There's encouragement here for us. We romanticise the first Christians so much we think they were perfect, that they had perfect faith without a hint of doubt. But these verses plainly show that that was not the case. Like Elijah, they were people with a nature like ours (James 5:17). But they prayed. And God answered even though they were slow to believe. Sometimes God answers our prayers, not because of our faith, but because of his grace. He often gives more than we deserve or expect.

The apostle Paul believed in praying for others. His letters are sprinkled with them; he moves easily and naturally from talking to his readers about God to talking to God about his readers. In turn he coveted the prayers of his churches, asking for prayer in every letter he wrote – except the letter to the backsliding Galatians.

Survival Rate of the Newborn

Pick a church – any church – and thumb through its membership roll. You may be surprised at the number of people on the roll who are never in church. At one time they were there, but not now, not for a long time maybe. Do you know someone like that? I'm sure you do. Christianity is littered with discarded disciples; membership rolls groan under the weight of Demases who have forsaken the Lord for the love of the world. We shake our heads and wonder what happened to them. Perhaps they weren't sincere to begin with. As a matter of fact, now that you mention it, I did have a reservation or two about that one – you know, his background and all.

But let me ask a question. Did we pray for that infant in the faith? When we first noticed signs of decay, when we began to suspect that the enemy had made a bridgehead in his new life – did we pray? Did we take the burden upon our own heart and bear them to the throne of grace to build a protective wall of prayer around him?

In many places the mortality rate of new-born believers is extremely high. Some do not live beyond the first year. Others live but never mature; they remain children all their lives.

The pain of childbirth is twofold: there is the pain of bringing the child into the world, and there is the pain of bringing that child up in the world. And the latter is greater. The physical pain of bearing a child is tremendous, but usually lasts only a few hours. But the pain of *rearing* that same child lasts a lifetime and never lessens. Lewis Smedes says, 'When you conceive a child, you covenant to suffer.'[1]

Paul knew the pain both of childbirth and of child-growth. Writing to the Galatians (the ones he *didn't* ask to pray for him), he said, 'O my dear children, I am suffering a mother's birth pang for you *again*, until Christ is formed in you' (Galatians 4:19, Williams, emphasis added). His parental concern shows itself in all his writings, especially Ephesians, Philippians and Colossians. He cradled his children in the arms of intercession.

A Good Work Begun, A Good Work Completed

I love Paul's words to his Philippian converts: 'Being confident of this very thing, that he who has begun a good work in you will complete it until the day of Jesus Christ' (Philippians 1:6). Would to God every pastor could say that about his churchmembers. But before the word of assurance in verse 6, Paul said something else in verses three and four: 'I thank my God upon every remembrance of you, always in every prayer of mine making request for you all with joy.' The intercession of verse 4 precedes the declaration of verse 6. Could there be a connection? Perhaps if we could say, 'I am always praying for you,' we could also say, 'I am confident that what God started in you he will complete.'

But Paul has something even more compelling to say to these believers. Philippians is a 'thank-you' note from Paul to the church at Philippi, thanking them for their much-welcomed gift (4:10) and assuring them that, although unjustly jailed by the authorities and unfairly treated by some of 'the brethren', he was doing great. As a matter of fact, rather than worrying about him, they should rejoice because all of this 'will turn out for my salvation through your prayer and the supply of the Spirit of Jesus Christ' (verse 19).

All these things, designed to harm Paul and hinder his work, will actually turn out for his 'spiritual welfare' (the meaning of 'salvation' here). Instead of thwarting his work, the circumstances are advancing it.

Paul's heart had been set on going to Rome. In Acts 19:21 he declared, 'I must see Rome.' And see Rome he did. But not the way he had planned. He expected to stride into the great city as an ambassador for Christ, unashamedly proclaiming the gospel. Instead he was led into Rome, dragging the chains of a prisoner. But this, he insists, has made his mission all the more successful – he has testified for his Lord in Caesar's palace, and 'it has become evident to the whole palace guard, and to all the rest, that my chains are in Christ' (verse 13). The adversities the Philippians were anxious about had actually turned out for the greater progress of the gospel. Paul's statement of faith is eloquent: 'I know that this will turn out for my salvation.'

Supplications and Supply

And then Paul tells them how this will be accomplished: 'through your prayer and the supply of the Spirit of Jesus Christ' (verse 19). God will use two instruments: 'your prayer' and the 'supply of the Spirit'.

Now stop and think about that. Let it sink in. It is not a new concept that the Spirit of God 'helps in our weaknesses' (Romans 8:26). We know about the supply of the Spirit. But what is this about 'your prayers'? It almost sounds like Paul is saying that the prayers of the Philippians are just as necessary to his deliverance as the supply of the Spirit. That is exactly what he is saying. Paul judges the prayers of the saints to be as essential as the provision of the Spirit. And I could point out that he mentions the prayers of the saints *first*. Did you know your prayers were that important?

'The prayer of the Philippians is not too unimportant,

not too human, not too impotent to stand next to that first Magnitude (the Holy Spirit), next to whom, strictly speaking, no second can stand.'[2]

Paul knew three things: he knew the Philippians were praying for him, he knew that when they received his letter, they would pray even more, and he knew that their prayers would bring the blessings of God upon him.

This same idea is found also in 2 Corinthians. Paul describes the burdens of his ministry as having 'the sentence of death in ourselves' (2 Corinthians 1:9); but he is confident that the God 'who delivered us from so great a death, and does deliver us; in whom we trust that he will still deliver us' (verse 10), '*you also helping together in prayer for us* . . .' (emphasis added).

God has chosen to work through his people – and through their prayers. And as far as these two passages are concerned, Paul believes the prayers of the saints are as important as the supply of the Spirit. Are they that important in our eyes?

God's Prayer List

Paul suggests that God has a prayer list when he writes to Timothy: 'Therefore I exhort first of all that supplications, prayers, intercessions, and giving of thanks be made for all men, for kings and all who are in authority, that we may lead a quiet and peaceable life in all godliness and reverence' (1 Timothy 2:1,2).

Paul is giving his young people a course in pastoral ministry, and the first thing you should do when your people come together, he says, is to pray. First on the agenda of worship – first, not in sequence necessarily, but first in importance: 'First of all'. Prayer is the supreme exercise of worship. The church can do nothing greater than this.

71

Pray For Secular Leaders

There are some surprises in this prayer list. First, Paul tells us to pray for *secular leaders*, 'for kings and all that are in authority'. Kings? Are we to pray for the king? That's the fellow who is slaughtering Christians as fast as the lions can eat them. Pray for him? Right, I'll pray for him – I'll ask God to dump fire and brimstone on his head.

But that is not what Paul has in mind. Paul's admonition here reflects his conviction that the secular state is instituted by God for the welfare of man. He enunciates this in his letter to the Romans: 'Let every soul be subject to the governing authorities. For there is no authority except from God, and the authorities that exist are appointed by God' (Romans 13:1).

And Peter, addressing believers under the menace of persecution, says, 'Therefore submit yourselves to every ordinance of man for the Lord's sake, whether to the king as supreme, or to governors, as to those who are sent by him for the punishment of evil doers and for the praise of those who do good. *For this is the will of God*, that by doing good you may put to silence the ignorance of foolish men' (1 Peter 2:13–15, emphasis added).

'All who are in authority' are those in places of prominence, high positions. The phrase embraces everyone in a position of authority over us – employers, school teachers, church leaders, as well as government officials.

A couple of points we should touch on are, first, the significance of Paul's use of the plural, 'kings'. Paul does not refer to the present king or emperor only, but to those who follow also – which makes this of permanent application to the church.

Second, Paul does not have in mind prayer primarily aimed at the king's conversion to Christ. Kings do not have to be Christian kings to be equitable and honourable rulers. Here Paul is thinking of prayer for them in their role as rulers, as men who carry heavy burdens of responsibility and exert powerful influence on the lives of citizens. God's providence is impartial, the rain falling on the just and the unjust, and so should be our prayers, praying even for those who spitefully use and persecute us (Matthew 5:44). Even non-Christian rulers need the support of our prayers, for no matter how wicked the rulers may be, anarchy is worse.

By praying for them, the church helps those in authority to exercise their powers wisely and justly. This is obvious as Paul unfolds the motive for such prayer: 'that we may lead a quiet and peaceable life in all godliness and reverence' (verse 2). When rulers rule properly their subjects can live quiet and peaceable lives, the opposite of which is unrest and disturbance, two words that graphically describe our present world.

Good rulers make good government, which in turn makes life quiet and peaceable for us, which in turn makes a favourable environment for preaching the gospel, and 'this is good and acceptable in the sight of God our Saviour, who desires all men to be saved and to come to the knowledge of the truth' (verses 3,4).

Pray for Spiritual Leaders

Some years ago I heard a visiting evangelist announce his sermon title for the following night: 'How To Fire Your Minister.' That was too tantalising to pass up; the next evening the building was packed. But groans of disappointment from the congregation and sighs of relief from a number of ministers filled the air when the evangelist revealed the secret: 'If you want to fire your preacher,' he thundered, 'Pray for him! Pray that the Holy Ghost will fall on him and set him afire!'

They called him a sensationalist, but he got his point across. If you don't like your minister, change him – by praying for him. Better praying in the pew might make better preaching in the pulpit.

God's Blessings on Their Public Ministry

One of the chief characteristics of Paul's letters are his constant appeals for the prayers of his converts. In Ephesians 6:18, he writes: 'Praying always with all prayer and supplication in the Spirit . . . for all the saints – *and for me*, that utterance may be given to me, that I may open my mouth boldly to make known the mystery of the gospel' (emphasis added).

Again in Colossians 4:3,6, 'Meanwhile praying also for us, that God would open to us a door for the word, to speak the mystery of Christ . . . that I may make it manifest, as I ought to speak.'

Christians should pray regularly for their pastors, evangelists and missionaries, that God would throw open doors of opportunity and enable them to preach Christ courageously and clearly.

God's Protection on Their Private Lives

Just a few hours ago I watched on television the sad spectacle of another high-profile minister stepping down from his pulpit amid charges of immoral conduct. He joins a growing number of fallen ministers. I do not believe these men are representative of most ministers of the gospel, but I have been in the ministry for more than thirty years, and while there have always been instances of moral failure, I've never seen anything like this. I have no doubt that the enemy has mounted a massive campaign to discredit preachers; like a roaring lion the devil is seeking to devour spiritual leaders, and many have been caught in his jaws.

Few people are as vulnerable to gossip and innuendo as are ministers. That's why Paul spurred the Thessalonian believers to hedge them about with protective intercession. 'Finally brothers, pray for us . . . that we may be delivered

74

from unprincipled and wicked men; for not all have faith'
(2 Thessalonians 3:1,2, Williams). Paul's request here for
prayer is emphatic and imperative, and the tense is
continuous. He is not asking to be remembered occasionally,
'as the Lord brings me to mind'. He is asking for
continuous and vigilant prayer support.

A word, a suspicion, a raised eyebrow – it takes little
more than this to destroy the ministry of a person and the
testimony of a church. Intercession can build a wall of
protection around our spiritual leaders. Such prayer
'produces what Raymond Johnston has called "an anti-
septic atmosphere," in which blasphemy, selfishness,
greed, dishonesty, immorality, cruelty and injustice find
it harder to flourish.'[3]

Praying With Paul

Much of our praying should be directed to building up
fellow believers. Again, Paul is our example; the prayers
preserved in his epistles show this was a concern of his
own prayer life. They provide a Spirit-inspired answer to
the question: 'How should I pray for other Christians?'

Believers need to realise their unlimited resources in
Christ. Listen to Paul pray: 'That the God of our Lord
Jesus Christ, the Father of glory may give to you the
spirit of wisdom and revelation in the knowledge of
him . . . that you may know what is the hope of his
calling, what are the riches of his glory of his inheritance
in the saints . . . the exceeding greatness of his power
toward us who believe' (Ephesians 1:17–19). Think
what that would mean to a believer about to go down for
the count before the tempter – to suddenly realise that
the same power that raised Jesus from the dead dwells in
him, and is available to him at that very moment. These
are the people we should pray for.

Ephesians 3:14–19 is a treasury of biblical petitions.
Paul bows his knees to the Father and prays that the

believers at Ephesus would be

Strengthened with might through his Spirit in the inner man,

that Christ may dwell in their hearts through faith,

that they would be able to know and comprehend the love of Christ, and *that they might be filled with the fullness of God*.

Another rich prayer catalogue is found in Philippians 1:9–11. Paul prays specifically for these Christians

that their *love may abound more and more,*

that they may *approve things that are excellent,*

that they may be *sincere and without offence,*

that they may be *filled with the fruits of righteousness.*

One more example – Colossians 1:9–12. Here Paul prays that the Colossian Christians

will be *filled with the knowledge of God's will,*

that they might *walk worthy of the Lord unto all pleasing,*

that they will be *fruitful in every good work,*

that they will *increase in the knowledge of God,*

that they will be *strengthened with all might,* and

that they will live a *life of continual thanksgiving.*

Some Suggested Supplications

Now let's scoop up these Pauline prayers, mix them together and draw out a list of scriptural supplications. Certain friends may come to mind as you read through the list. They may be the ones you should pray for first.

When you pray for others, pray that

1. Their eyes would be open to their unlimited resources in Christ.
2. They will be strengthened by the Holy Spirit.
3. They will be filled with all the fullness of God.
4. They will fully understand and appreciate the love of Christ.
5. Their love for others would grow to overflowing.

6. They will be able to discern right from wrong and make the right decisions in all matters.
7. They will be free of all pretence and hypocrisy and live a blameless life.
8. Their life will be full of the future of righteousness.
9. They will know God's will for their lives and be committed to it.
10. They will please the Lord in everything they do.
11. They will be fruitful in every good work.
12. They will hunger and thirst to know more and more about God.

This list, of course, is not a string of prayer beads to chant over the names of the people you pray for. These are suggestions, scriptural suggestions, and you will phrase and reword them according to the needs of those on your prayer list.

Remember God works through our prayers to bring the supply of the Spirit into the lives of needy believers. By praying for others we can bring to bear the power of Jesus into a person's life. We can apply his healing power to wounded hearts. We can say with Paul that we are confident of this very thing, that he who began a good work in these will complete it until the day of Jesus Christ. And we also, helping by our prayers.

In 1650 Jeremy Taylor wrote a book called *The Rules and Exercises of Holy Living*. He said this about prayer.

Christ hath put it (the power of prayer) into the hands of men, and the prayers of men have saved cities and kingdoms from ruin; prayer hath raised dead men to life, hath stopped the violence of fire, shut the mouths of wild beasts, altered the course of nature, caused rain in Egypt and drought in the sea. Prayer rules over all gods; it arrests the sun in its course and stays the chariot wheels of the moon; it reconciles our suffering and weak faculties with the violence of torment and the violence of persecution; it pleases God and supplies all our need.

77

6: Praying For The Lost

A few years ago I was invited to give a series of lectures on prayer at a well-known evangelical seminary. At their request I sent manuscripts of each of the five messages I would deliver, including one titled, 'Praying for the Lost'. Several weeks later I received a letter from a member of the chapel lecture committee asking if I would substitute another message in place of the one on praying for the lost, which, of course, I did. It was the stated position of the seminary president that praying for the lost to be saved was unscriptural. I've always regretted that he and I didn't have a chance to discuss it, because I believe it was largely a matter of semantics.

Can We Pray For The Lost?

The prayer of Jesus in John 17 is often pointed to as evidence that we are not to pray for the lost. In his prayer, Jesus said, 'I ask on their behalf, I do not ask on behalf of the world, but of those whom thou hast give me; for they are thine' (verse 9 NAS). But this is arguing from inference. At that moment Jesus was praying for his followers only, not for the world. But there is no suggestion that the world was never to be prayed for; at that precise moment in that specific prayer Jesus did not pray for the world, but he did not say we should never pray for the world. Only a few hours later Jesus prayed for a part of that lost world when he cried on the cross, 'Father, forgive them, for they know not what they do.'

The apostle Paul saw no problem in praying for the unsaved Jews: 'Brethren, my heart's desire and my prayer to God for them is for their salvation' (Romans 10:1 NAS).

In 1 John 5:14,15, we have this promise: 'Now this is the confidence that we have in him, that if we ask anything according to his will, he hears us: and if we know that he hears us, whatever we ask, we know that we have the petitions that we have asked of him.'

Couple that promise with these statements: 'The Lord is not slack concerning his promise, as some men count slackness; but is longsuffering toward us, not willing that any should perish but that all should come to repentance' (2 Peter 3:9).

'Who (God) desires all men to be saved and to come to the knowledge of the truth' (1 Timothy 2:4).

The will of God is clearly stated in these verses. Christ's death on the cross established the fact that God is not willing that any should perish. When we pray for the lost to be saved, we are praying within the revealed will of God. To say that we may not pray for the lost to be saved is to deny ourselves the mightiest power God has given us to accomplish our greatest task.

God has always used intercessors to achieve his will. Intercession has postponed, even prevented the wrath of God from coming upon an individual or a nation. In Job 42, God told Eliphaz and his two friends to go to Job and let him pray for them, 'lest I deal with you according to your folly' (Job 42:8). We have already seen that the intercession of Moses saved his nation from the judgement of God. When God destroyed Sodom and Gomorrah, he spared Lot because he remembered Abraham's intercession.

The four men who lowered their crippled friend through the ceiling to get to Jesus, were 'intercessors'. The Bible says, 'When he (Jesus) saw their faith, he said unto him (the man sick of the palsy), man, your sins are forgiven you' (Luke 5:20). Jesus saw *their* faith. Whether the sick man had faith is not mentioned. But it was the faith of his friends that secured the healing.

The simple, yet profound fact is that God responds to prayer. Because we pray he does things that he would not otherwise do (See Chapter Two). That God would place such incomparable privilege and responsibility in our hands is past understanding. But he has done just that. Through intercession we can become the instrument of salvation to men and women we never see face to face in this life. We can become in one moment a missionary to the farthest corners of the earth. With the arms of intercession we can embrace the world and lift it to God in prayer.

Seeking and Saving

What did Jesus mean when he said, 'For the Son of Man has come to seek and to save that which was lost' (Luke 19:10)? It must mean 'more than a mere attempt to locate unsaved men, for they are present on every hand. The term ... suggests a divine preparation of the unsaved that will bring them into adjustment with the necessary conditions of salvation.'[1]

Divine Preparation of the Unsaved

This is seen in the episode of Philip and the Ethiopian eunuch (Acts 8:26–40). The Ethiopian was returning from Jerusalem where he had gone to worship, and sitting in his chariot, he was reading about the Suffering Servant in Isaiah. At that precise moment, Philip, obeying the Spirit, joined the man and asked if he understood what he was reading. Now that's what I call preparation. Before Philip ever saw the Ethiopian, before the Spirit ever told him to join the man, God had been preparing his heart to hear about Jesus. And when he was ready, God dispatched Philip to complete the task.

And the same was true of Cornelius, the centurion (Acts 10:1 ff). Only after he was prepared to hear the gospel did God summon Peter. Cornelius was ready to be saved before Peter was ready to tell him how.

Preparation *for* salvation is part of the work *of* salvation. To the Thessalonians, Paul said, 'But we are bound to give thanks to God always for you, brethren beloved by the Lord, because God from the beginning chose you for salvation through sanctification by the Spirit and belief in the truth' (2 Thessalonians 2:13). Notice the order of the clauses: chosen for salvation through sanctification and belief in the truth. Shouldn't belief in the gospel precede sanctification of the Spirit?

But here sanctification comes before salvation because Paul isn't referring to the sanctification of believers but to the sanctification of sinners. This is the work of the Spirit in which he draws a circle around a lost person, sets him apart, and says, in effect, 'It's your time.'

A college student, professing to be an atheist, once wrote to C. S. Lewis, explaining that he had fallen in with some Christian students who were vigorously witnessing to him of their faith. Some of the things they said had unsettled his thinking; he was going through some great struggles. What did Dr Lewis think? Lewis wrote back: 'I think you are already in the meshes of the net – the Holy Spirit is after you. I doubt you will get away.'

Salvation does not realise itself immediately. 'The chariot of fire does not come down and snatch away one after another to glory.'[2]

We find a similar thought in 1 Peter 1:2. Peter, addressing the pilgrims of the dispersion, describes them as the 'elect according to the foreknowledge of God the Father, in sanctification of the Spirit, for obedience and sprinkling of the blood of Jesus Christ'. Again the order of the clauses is significant: 'elect . . . in sanctification of the Spirit *for* obedience and sprinkling of the blood'.

81

We would assume that obedience and sprinkling of the blood would precede sanctification. But again, it appears that Peter is referring to a sanctification that brings about salvation, rather than a sanctification of the believer that follows salvation. And intercession plays a major role in this divine drama of preparation.

Here are some things that will help us as we pray for the lost. They are the context in which we intercede.

The Condition of the Sinner

The lost person is bound by the god of this world. Whether we evangelise through preaching or through praying, we must reckon with this fact. Let's look at some relevant passages.

'With gentleness he must correct his opponents, for God might grant them repentance that would lead them to a full knowledge of the truth, and they might recover their senses and *escape from the devil's trap in which they have been caught by him to do his will*' (2 Timothy 2:25,26 Williams, emphasis added). Men have been 'taken alive' (the meaning of the Greek verb) by Satan and as his captives they are slaves to his will. The only hope for them is that God may grant them repentance.

Paul writes: 'In which you once walked according to the course of this world, *according to the prince of the power of the air*, the spirit who now *works in the sons of disobedience*' (Ephesians 2:2 emphasis added). The word translated 'works' here is literally 'energised', and is used elsewhere of the Holy Spirit's activity in the believer. The unsaved person is energised by the spirit of the devil. Of course, a lost person doesn't know that, and certainly would not admit it if he did. He thinks he is free (that's part of his lostness), but in truth his course of action is dictated by the prince of the power of the air.

And in 1 John: 'We know that we are of God, and the whole world lies in the power of the evil one' (1 John 5:19, NAS).

The Greek verb translated 'lies' conveys the picture of a mother cradling her baby in her arms and rocking it to sleep. That is a vivid picture of the lost – cradled in the arms of Satan, helplessly and hopelessly lulled to sleep.

Jesus said, 'When a strong man well armed keeps guard over his dwelling, *his property is secure*. But when a man stronger than he attacks him and overcomes him, he strips him of all his arms on which he relied, and distributes his goods as spoils' (Luke 11:21,22 Williams, emphasis added).

In this passage Jesus is answering the charge that he casts out demons by Beelzebub, the ruler of demons (Luke 11:14 ff). Two things are especially noteworthy in his reply. One, men are described as the property of Satan, who stands guard over them lest they should escape.

Two, before he can free the captives, Jesus must first deal with the captor, Satan, and disarm him. We will do well to keep that in mind.

In praying for a lost person, we are not forcing his will – we are *freeing* his will from the bondage of Satan.

The lost person is also blind to the gospel. Listen to Paul, 'But even if our gospel is veiled, it is veiled to those who are perishing, *whose minds the god of this age has blinded*, who do not believe, lest the light of the gospel of the glory of Christ, who is the image of God, should shine on them' (2 Corinthians 4:3,4 emphasis added).

An unsaved person does not have the capacity to see himself as a lost sinner or to understand the gospel message. He has been blinded spiritually. Paul tells us that 'the natural man does not receive the things of the Spirit of God, for they are foolishness to him: nor can he know them, because they are spiritually discerned' (1 Corinthians 2:14).

No amount of human power, logic or argument can penetrate the darkness of the unsaved mind. We cannot explain the way of salvation simply enough for him to believe. The devil doesn't have to make a drunkard or a murderer of a person to keep them from being saved. He has only to blind him to the gospel of Christ.

In summary a lost person is *bound by the god of this world*, and *blind to the gospel of Christ*. Before any person can be saved two things must occur: the binding and blinding of the devil must be overcome. There must be emancipation and enlightenment. As we saw earlier, Jesus had first to deal with the devil before he could free the captives.

In a sense, the primary target in evangelism is not the sinner, but Satan. We are engaged in spiritual warfare and we must meet the devil on his own ground. Paul tells us that our conflict is not with flesh and blood, but with the unholy powers of spiritual darkness (Ephesians 6:12). In his letter to the Corinthians, he says that we do not fight this war with weapons of flesh, but with the mighty weapons of God (2 Corinthians 10:3,4). Our warfare is not physical and material and our weapons cannot be physical and material weapons.

The church has always been slow to learn this. We wade into battle armed with beautiful buildings and carefully planned programmes and high-powered publicity. These things are good, but alone they are useless in spiritual warfare. We must get beyond the material to the spiritual.

Jesus had a way of getting past the surface problem to the power behind the problem. Peter, after making his great declaration concerning the identity of Jesus, proceeded to rebuke the Lord for his talk of going to Jerusalem to die. How did Jesus respond? Did he appeal to Peter's understanding of the scriptures or present a logical reason for going to Jerusalem? No, Jesus went beyond the problem to the power behind the problem and said, 'Get behind Me, Satan!' (Matthew 16:23). Jesus knew that his conflict was not with the flesh and blood of Simon Peter, but with the spiritual powers of darkness.

When Paul and Silas were in Philippi, a young fortune teller followed them for many days, crying, 'These men are the servants of the Most High God, who proclaim to us the way of salvation' (Acts 16:17,18). How did the apostle deal with this? Did he inform the girl of the dangers of occultism and challenge her to forsake her misguided ways? On the contrary, the Bible says he turned to her and said *to the spirit*, 'I command you in the name of Jesus Christ to come out of her' (Acts 16:18). Paul went beyond the problem to the power behind the problem. His warfare was spiritual and he used spiritual weapons.

This is where intercession enters the picture. Mark Chapter 9 tells the story of the demon-possessed boy and his father. While Jesus is on the mountain with Peter, James and John, the remaining disciples attempt unsuccessfully to cast the demon out of the boy. After Jesus arrived on the scene and delivered the boy, his disciples began 'questioning him privately, "Why is it that we could not cast it out?" And he said to them, "This kind cannot come out by anything but prayer"' (Mark 9:28,29 NAS).

Where's the War?

Ephesians Chapter 6 sheds a great deal of light on this subject. 'Finally, my brethren, be strong in the Lord and in the power of his might. Put on the whole armour of God, that you may be able to stand against the wiles of the devil. For we do not wrestle against flesh and blood, but against principalities, against powers, against the rulers of the darkness of this age, against spiritual hosts of wickedness in the heavenly places' (Ephesians 6:10–12).

The Christian life is a life of warfare. Five times in this passage Paul uses the word *against*. The Christian is against something. Paul says that we *wrestle*, a Greek word meaning 'hand-to-hand combat'. It is a personal battle, not spectator sport viewed from a safe distance. We are in the thick of it, personally involved in this conflict, whether we know it or not.

If we are to wage successfully this spiritual battle we must have spiritual armour and spiritual weapons; Paul tells us what we need in verses 13–17:

> Therefore take up the whole armour of God, that you may be able to withstand in the evil day, and having done all, to stand. Stand therefore, having girded your waist with truth, having put on the breastplate of righteousness, and having shod your feet with the preparation of the gospel of peace; above all, taking the shield of faith . . . the helmet of salvation, and the sword of the Spirit, which is the word of God.

Now let's follow Paul closely. First, he tells us that there really is a war, a spiritual war, requiring spiritual equipment. Then he tells us to suit up for the fight – put on the whole armour of God, arm yourself with the sword of the Spirit. All right, here I am, Paul: I'm dressed and ready to go. I have on the helmet of salvation, I'm holding this big body shield of faith; the belt of truth is buckled tightly to support me and hold the other pieces of armour in place. My feet are shod with the readiness to obey God; I've got the sword. Now, where's the war? I'm ready to fight, point me in the direction of the battle.

And he does: 'praying always with all prayer and supplication . . .' (verse 18). Is he serious? I've made intense preparation, I'm wearing an iron suit and wielding this giant sword, and what does Paul tell me to do? *Pray.*

Go back to verse 14. It begins, 'Stand therefore, having . . .'. The command is to 'stand'; the rest of verse 14 and all of verses 15 through 17 are parenthetical; we get back on the main track at verse 18 – 'praying always with all prayer and supplication . . .'. Drop everything between the 'therefore' of verse 14 and the 'praying' of verse 18, and you have: 'Stand therefore praying always with all prayer and supplication.' *Prayer is the warfare. It is the battlefield upon which the spiritual war is fought.* The battle is won and lost here.

Before we ever step on to the battlefield of preaching or teaching or witnessing, the battle has already been decided on the battlefield of prayer. This is vividly portrayed in Exodus 17. The Israelites meet Amalek in the Valley of Rephidim; he blocks the path of Israel and says, 'This is as far as you go. If you go any further it will be over my dead body.'

Moses says to Joshua, 'You get your men and go down into the valley and fight Amalek, and I'll get on top of the mountain and hold up the rod of God.' I think if I had been Joshua I might have said, 'Moses – I've got a better idea. *You* go down in the valley and I'll get up on the mountain.'

But Joshua followed Moses' orders and fought Amalek in the valley. Meanwhile, Moses is on the mountain, with the rod of God, and a strange thing happens. When Moses holds up the rod, Joshua prevails; when he lowers the rod, Amalek prevails. Like a symphony orchestra, the battle follows the baton of the maestro. But Moses tires and his hands become leadweights, and on the mountain, the rod of God sinks, and in the valley, Amalek prevails.

But Aaron and Hur are with Moses on the mountain; they find a stone for Moses to sit on, then, one or either side of him, they hold up Moses' hands 'until the going down of the sun'. And Joshua prevails. I love the understatement of the old King James version: 'Joshua discomfited Amalek and his people with the edge of the sword' (Exodus 17:13).

Where was the battle decided? In the valley with Joshua? No, it was decided on the mountain with Moses. The victory in the valley is won by the intercession on the mountain. The church could win more battles in the valley if it had more intercessors on the mountain lifting high the name of Jesus.

The battle for lost souls is won by prayer and intercession. Prayer *is* the warfare. Evangelism is going out on to the field of victory and gathering up the spoils of victory. Evangelism is not an attempt to win the battle – the battle has already been won through prayer; evangelism is the mopping-up operation. The physical possessions of the church, the buildings, organisations and programmes are the trucks we drive on to the battlefield to load up the spoils of victory won by intercession.

This leads to the next truth we should understand in praying for the lost:

The Conquest of Satan

The New Testament clearly teaches that the devil is a defeated enemy. His defeat is twofold. First, it is *absolute*. We've already seen in Luke 11 that Jesus has bound the strong man, the devil. Another helpful passage is Hebrews 2:14,15: 'Since then the children share in flesh and blood, he himself likewise also partook of the same, that through death he might render powerless him who had the power of death, that is, the devil; and might deliver those who through fear of death were subject to slavery all their lives' (NAS).

Another passage says, 'He who sins is of the devil, for the devil has sinned from the beginning. For this purpose the Son of God was manifested, that he might destroy the works of the devil' (1 John 3:8).

We read in Colossians that Christ has 'cancelled out the certificate of debt consisting of decrees against us and which was hostile to us; and he has taken it out of the way, having nailed it to the cross. When he had disarmed the rulers and authorities, he made a public display of them, having triumphed over them through him' (Colossians 2:14,15 NAS).

The language of this verse is taken from the victory march of the conquering Roman generals. After defeating an enemy, the victorious commander would chain the officers of the defeated army to his chariot and drag them back to the city of Rome. He sent a runner ahead to announce to the city that the victory had been won, and the people lined the streets awaiting the spectacle. By the way, do you know what that runner was doing? He was preaching. He was heralding the good news of victory. The same Greek word for a 'herald', a proclaimer, an announcer is used to describe preaching. The herald wasn't winning the victory, he was announcing a victory that had already been won. And that's what preaching and witnessing are – announcing the good news of a victory already won.

Finally, the triumphant train entered the city – trumpets blaring, citizens cheering, garlands streaming – the conquering hero in his chariot drawn by magnificent white stallions, and trailing behind, chained to the chariot that was moving slightly faster than they could run, thus stumbling, falling, dragged in the dust, were the leaders of the defeated army. The victor not only conquered the enemy, he made a public spectacle of them.

When Jesus died on the cross, he defeated Satan and all his thugs. And when he burst forth from the grave, he made a public spectacle of them. Satan's defeat is absolute.

Well, you may ask, if that's so, then why do I have such a hard time with him? If the devil is chained, he either has a mighty long chain, or he's chained to me. Has anyone informed Satan of his defeat? He acts like he doesn't know it. It's a good question, and there is a good answer.

Although Satan's defeat is absolute, for the time being, until God rings down the curtain on history, his defeat must be *appropriated*. This is true of everything God has done for us through Christ. What God has made available we must appropriate.[3]

Look at Matthew 18:18: 'Truly I say to you, whatever you shall bind on earth shall have been bound in heaven; and whatever you loose on earth shall have been loosed in heaven' (NAS). We are to take our cue from heaven. Whatever has already been bound in heaven, we may bind on earth; whatever has already been loosed in heaven, we may loose on earth. We are to see things from heaven's viewpoint. Now, from heaven's viewpoint, has Satan been bound? Yes. From heaven's viewpoint, have slaves of Satan been loosed? Yes. Absolutely.

James provides a perfect illustration of this: 'Therefore submit to God. Resist the devil and he will flee from you' (James 4:7).

Now, let's catch up with ourselves. So far we have said: one, the unsaved are bound in slavery and blind to the gospel; two, it is the devil who has done this; three, before anyone can be saved, they must first be emancipated and enlightened; and four, the devil who has bound them and blinded them has been defeated absolutely by Christ and rendered powerless.

The Cross of Christ

The atonement of Christ is the main pillar upon which intercession rests. In 1 John 2:1,2, we read, 'My little children, these things I write to you, that you may not sin. And if anyone sins, we have an Advocate with the Father, Jesus Christ the righteous. And he himself is the propitiation for our sins, and not for ours only but also for the whole world.'

Propitiation means 'atoning sacrifice' or 'covering'. On the cross, Jesus covered our sins with his blood, and not our sins only, but 'also for the whole world'. He is the 'Lamb of God, who takes away the sin of the whole world!' (John 1:29). The sins of the whole world have been paid for by the sacrifice of Christ. At this point someone may say, 'But I believe in a limited atonement'. Even so, the principle is the same: the basis on which the elect are saved is the atoning work of Christ.

Men do not go to hell because of their sins, they go to hell because they reject the atonement made by Christ. 'For God did not send his Son into the world to condemn the world, but that the world through him might be saved. He who believes in him is not condemned; but he who does not believe in him is condemned already *because he has not believed in the name of the only begotten Son of God*' (John 3:17,18 emphasis added).

Why is the lost person condemned? Is it because he steals, or curses, or gets drunk? No. He is not condemned by what he has done, he is condemned by what *he has not done*. He has not believed.

In the book of Revelation we find a picture of the final judgment of the unsaved dead.

> And I saw the dead, small and great, standing before God, and books were opened. And another book was opened, which is the Book of Life. And the dead were judged according to their works, by the things which were written in the books. The sea gave up the dead who were in it, and Death and Hades delivered up the dead who were in them. And they were judged each one according to his works . . . . And anyone *not found written in the Book of Life* was cast into the lake of fire (Revelation 20:13,14,15 emphasis added).

Observe that while the unsaved dead are judged according to their works, they are not cast into the lake of fire because of those works. The books of works are opened to prove their need of salvation. They are cast into the lake of fire, not because of what was written in the books of works, but because of what was *not written* in the Book of Life – their names. Regardless of how bad their record was, if their names had been written in the Book of Life, they would have escaped eternal punishment.

Our right to pray for the lost is based on the fact that Christ has already paid for their sin with his blood. We are claiming what is rightly his.

One week in December when I was in seminary in Fort Worth, Texas, I preached at a Bible conference in Florida. My wife and two-year-old son visited her parents in Arkansas. On my way home from Florida, I picked them up in Arkansas and we arrived in Fort Worth on a freezing December afternoon. When we walked into the house, we found that it was just as cold inside as it was outside. It didn't take long to discover that our gas had been cut off. With my little family standing there shivering, I picked up the phone and called the gas company and asked them what in the world was going on. We were freezing to death, for heaven's sake.

A voice, as icy as the weather, replied, 'Mr Dunn, you failed to pay last month's bill. We couldn't get hold of you so we cut off your gas.'

'But I paid it,' I said.

'I'm sorry, but we have no record of any payment,' the icy voice said. 'You will have to come down to the office and pay the bill before we can turn the gas back on.'

'Hang on a minute,' I said. I put the phone down and began searching through my desk for the stub that had the gas company's stamp on it – the one that says, PAID. And I found it. Grasping the proof of payment, I jerked up the receiver and told the icy voice to turn my gas back on, and do it now. And they did.

When Christ poured out his blood, he paid the ransom for lost souls, and when God raised him from the grave on the third day, he stamped the bill, *Paid in full*.

There will be times, as you pray for someone God has laid on your heart, you will hear an icy voice saying, 'You have no right to pray for him. He's my property. He belongs to me.'

But you can point to the proof of payment, the death and resurrection of Christ, and inform the icy voice that God has plundered his house and spoiled his goods. The Lord has foreclosed on the devil and bought up all his property.

What I have tried to say in this chapter is that when we pray for the lost in the name of Jesus we are laying claim to what Jesus has already paid for with his blood. 'Without any doubt we may assure the conversion of those laid on our hearts by such praying. The prayer in Jesus' Name drives the enemy off the battlefield of man's will and leaves him free to choose right.'[4]

7: The Life That Can Pray

Two things determine the answer to any prayer: first, the *prayer* must be according to the will of God. Regardless of how earnestly we believe or how desperately we cry out to God, any petition that lies outside the boundaries of his will is doomed to failure. Prayer is not a means of getting man's will done in heaven; it is the means of getting God's will done on earth.

Second, the *pray-er* must be according to the will of God. By pray-er, I mean the person who is praying. It is the life that prays. Prayer is as much *position* as it is petition. The prayer life rests upon the pray-er's life, and if that is weak, the prayer life will collapse.

When we try to explain prayer, we raise as many questions as we answer. There is so much we can't know. But this much we do know: for an effective prayer life, *being* is more important than *doing*. If I am qualified to pray (we're going to discuss that in a moment), the Holy Spirit will see to it that I learn how. But if my life is wrong, even the Holy Spirit cannot make me an intercessor.

It is the Life that Prays

Robert Murray McCheyene said, 'What a man is in his prayer-closet is what he is.' No Christian is greater than his prayer life. I'm not saying we have to be super-saints or heroes of holiness, but we cannot divorce our living from our praying.

It is possible to preach without being right with God. Preaching is a person-to-person encounter. We can teach a Sunday school class or even witness to a lost person without being right with God. These are person-to-person encounters. But prayer is a person-to-God encounter. It is an audience with one to whom all things are open and naked. We can't fake it with him. What we are when we are alone with God is what we are. It is 'the effective, fervent prayer of a righteous man' that avails much (James 5:16).

The Psalmist said, 'If I had cherished sin in my heart, the Lord would not have listened' (Psalm 66:18 NIV). To cherish iniquity means to look upon it with favour, to give it a place.

The apostle John expressed it like this: 'And whatever we ask we receive from him, because we keep his commandments and do those things that are pleasing in his sight' (1 John 3:22).

Christ's Order of Worship

I speak in a different church every week and when I arrive on Sunday morning, the first thing I look for is the Order of Worship printed in the Sunday bulletin. They're all pretty much the same – an organ prelude, an anthem by the choir, followed by the invocation. I've often wondered how we would fare using the Lord's Order of Worship. Which is:

> Therefore if you bring your gift to the altar, and there remember that your brother has something against you, leave your gift there before the altar, and go your way. First, be reconciled to your brother, and then come and offer your gift (Matthew 5:23,24).

This is Christ's Order of Worship: first, be reconciled to your brother.

Imagine the chaos in church on Sunday morning if every member of the choir refused to sing until they made things right with their brother. What if the organist said, 'I can't play yet, I've got to leave my gift here and, first, get right with my neighbour'? And what if the pastor said, 'I can't offer my gift of preaching at this altar until I have, first, made things right with my deacons'?

Probably the morning worship service wouldn't get underway until around four o'clock Monday afternoon, but when it did, it would be 'something else'.

What is the principle that Jesus gives us here? This: the quality of the gift is determined by the quality of the giver. Or we can put it like this: *the acceptability of any act of worship is determined by the acceptability of the worshipper*. The gestures of worship are meaningless if the heart isn't right.

This is powerfully enforced by Micah the prophet. In the midst of a fiery controversy with the Lord, Israel says, 'With what shall I come before the Lord, and bow myself before the High God?' And then they offer answers to their own question: 'Shall I come before him with burnt offerings, with calves of a year old?' This is what is expected. But they go beyond that. 'Will the Lord be pleased with thousands of rams or ten thousand rivers of oil?' Only a king could bring such an offering. This is an extravagant offering. The Lord will be impressed.

But the would-be-worshipper does not stop there. 'Shall I give my firstborn for my transgression, the fruit of my body for the sin of my soul?' Not even God would doubt the sincerity of such an extreme sacrifice. God is a tough negotiator, but Israel will meet his demands, whatever they are. Tell us what great thing we can do?

Then Micah flings the answer at them: 'He has showed you, O man, what is good; and what does the Lord require of you but to do justly, to love mercy, and to walk humbly with your God?' (Micah 6:6–8). Not even the sacrifice of the firstborn child can substitute for plain old honesty, kindness and humility. The acceptability of the gift is determined by the acceptability of the giver.

When I stand to preach, God looks at my heart before he listens to my sermon. If the heart is unacceptable, so is the sermon. The same is true with every activity of the Christian life, and especially in the matter of prayer.

Paul told Timothy he wanted 'the men everywhere to offer prayer, lifting to heaven holy hands which are kept unstained by anger and dissensions' (1 Timothy 2:8, Williams). Lifting up the hands was one of the three basic postures of praying among the Jews: kneeling, lying prostrate and standing with hands lifted to heaven. The emphasis here is not on 'hands' but on *holiness*. Paul could just as well have said, 'Kneel on *holy* knees'. The central concern here, as always in the New Testament, is not the mechanics or gestures of worship, but the attitude of the heart and the altitude of the life. Remember, it is the life that prays.

So, what kind of life can pray? Jesus tells us in John 15:7: 'If you abide in me, and my words abide in you, you will ask what you desire, and it shall be done for you.'

Meet the *normal* prayer life: 'You will ask what you will, and it shall be done for you.' This is from the same Bible that tells us we must pray 'according to the will of God' (1 John 5:14). Jesus is speaking of a life of such quality, lived in such a dimension, where the will of the believer so harmonises with the will of God that for him to 'ask what he will' is synonymous with asking 'according to his will.'

But this kind of praying flows from this kind of living: 'Abide in me, and my words abide in you.'

A Life of Abiding

Admittedly, 'abide' is not a word we use a great deal today. It's a little musty. To appreciate what Jesus is saying, we need some background.

As Jesus and his disciples made their way through the moonlit night from the upper room to the Garden of

Gethsemane, Jesus continued his 'upper room' discourse. Perhaps as they passed the Temple of Herod, Jesus paused to gaze at the emblem of the vine that adorned the monumental entrance. The vine was the national symbol, but Israel had become a 'dead vine'.

Jesus said, 'I am the true vine.' Actually Jesus said, 'I am the vine, the true one.' He is not one vine among others; he is the *true* vine, not necessarily as opposed to false, but, in the words of F. B. Meyer, 'true in the sense of real, substantial, and enduring: the essential, as distinguished from the circumstantial; the eternal, as distinct from the temporary and transient'.

In John 15, Jesus uses the figure of the vine and its branches to describe his relationship with the disciples. I am to you, he tells the disciples, what the vine is to the branches.

I am the true vine, and my Father is the vinedresser. Every branch in me that does not bear fruit he takes away; and every branch that bears fruit he prunes, that it may bear more fruit. You are already clean because of the word which I have spoken to you. Abide in me, and I in you. As the branch cannot bear fruit of itself, unless it abides in the vine, neither can you, unless you abide in me.

I am the vine, you are the branches. He who abides in me, and I in him, bears much fruit; for without me you can do nothing. If anyone does not abide in me, he is cast forth as a branch and is withered; and they gather them and throw them into the fire, and they are burned. If you abide in me, and my words abide in you, you will ask what you desire, and it shall be done for you. By this is my Father glorified, that you bear much fruit; so you will be my disciples (John 15:1-8).

Simply put, we are to be to Jesus what a branch is to a vine. As the branch abides in the vine, we are to abide in Jesus. The word, 'abide', speaks of the union and communion between the vine and the branches. To abide in Jesus is to live the life of a branch. Branch living involves several things.

First, the branch must accept the vine's purpose for its existence. That purpose is stated in verses 2 and 16: 'Every branch in me that does not bear fruit he [the Father] takes away.' 'You did not choose me, but I chose you and appointed you that you should go and bear fruit, and that your fruit should remain, that whatever you ask the Father in my name he may give you.'

Obviously, the purpose of the branch is to bear fruit. In itself it has no value. I love grapes but I've never eaten a grape's branch. The fact is, apart from bearing fruit, the branch cannot justify its existence. The wood of the vine is worthless, good for nothing; it can't even be used as fuel. In Old Testament times, people were instructed to bring sacrifices of wood to the Temple for the altar fires, any kind of wood – except the wood of the vine. It's too soft to be used for timber and there is little beauty in it. The branches were so useless that when they were pruned from the vine, they were piled in a heap and burned. The branch is good for one thing only – bearing fruit.

And did you notice that Jesus said, 'Every branch in me that *bears* fruit.' The branch does not produce the fruit, it bears the fruit. It is the vine that produces the fruit and the branch is what God uses to hang the grapes on. The branch is just a grape rack.

This is what it means to abide – patiently resting in Christ, confident that he, the vine, will produce the fruit. A healthy branch will bear fruit. The responsibility for producing fruit is not upon us, the branches; that is the responsibility of Christ, the vine. Our part is to be healthy branches, living in union and communion with him, so we can *bear* the fruit he produces.

This goes right along with what we saw in Chapter One. The 'greater works' of believers are actually the works of Jesus performed through their prayerful availability.

Several years ago my wife and I attended the annual meeting of our denomination in Portland, Oregon. When our convention closed, we had a couple of days free before going home, so we looked for another convention to attend. Fortunately for us, the F.P.A. (FruitPickers of America) was holding its annual convention right there in Portland. I was surprised at the similarity of the two meetings. Like ours, the F.P.A. convention had lots of booths and exhibits, displaying the most advanced instruments for picking fruit, the latest techniques in fruitpicking, various sizes and shapes of fruit baskets – things like that. There were a lot of speeches, too. We sat through all of them. I especially liked the one on 'Fruitpicking Burnout'.

But the last one was the best. It was delivered by the man who had led the convention in fruitpicking the previous year. The guy was a dynamic speaker and by the end of his message he had everyone on their feet, resolving they would pick more fruit than ever before. Inspired beyond their ability, the conventioneers grabbed baskets and rushed out to pick fruit.

We waited around. In a few hours the fruitpickers began to drift back in, passionless, joyless – and fruitless. Every basket was empty. Immediately a task force was formed to discover why, with the latest methods and the finest tools, their fruitpicking crusade failed. We couldn't stay around for the official report, but we heard about it some time later. It seemed they had devoted all their time and energy to fruitpicking and none to fruit*bearing*. They forgot that you have to *bear* fruit before you can pick it.

So here is the first essential in branch life: acknowledging that the purpose for which Christ saved us is fruitbearing. As the vine manifests its life through the branch, so Jesus manifests his life through us. The Christian is a branch on which God wants to hang a Christ-like life.

Which is what the fruit of the Christian is – a Christ-like life. *Fruit is the outward expression of the inward nature.*

I know people who can look at the leaf of a tree and immediately know what kind of tree it is. I can't do that. I need to see fruit. When I see an apple growing out of the branch of a tree, I know that is an apple tree. That little red apple hanging from that branch is the outward expression of the inward nature of that tree.

In the same way, Christ is the inward nature of the Christian, and if we are in union with him we will bear fruit. Our part is to abide.

A subtle progression of fruitfulness can be seen in Jesus' words. In verse 2, he speaks of a branch that *bears* fruit, then it is pruned to bear *more* fruit. And finally in verse 5, Jesus says that 'he who abides in me, and I in him, bears *much* fruit.' This progression should not be overlooked, for just as the vinedresser wants his vine to produce more and more fruit, Jesus wants us to bear more and more fruit. You and I can bear more fruit than we are bearing now. We have not reached our potential, and the Vinedresser intends that we should.

How does he go about making us more fruitful? Not by adding more branches – which is usually what we do when we want to be more fruitful. As a pastor, I have done that, thinking if we added more activities we would grow more fruitful – but we just grew weary. The problem is we think it's up to us to produce the fruit. But it is not more branches that make the vine more fruitful; it is *healthier* branches.

Having accepted the Vine's purpose for my life, I now make myself *available to that purpose*.

Have you ever watched a branch? It's not very exciting. It just sits there, doing nothing but resting in its appointed place, never isolated from its source of life. It 'abides'.

I'm not suggesting that abiding in Christ means that we sit down and do nothing. Abiding in Christ is not idling in Christ. Jesus was able to do what he did because he was constantly abiding in the Father, yet no one could accuse Jesus of idleness or passivity. The writer of Hebrews says that 'he who has entered in his (God's) rest has himself also ceased from his works as God did from his' (Hebrews 4:10). He doesn't say that he has ceased from work, just from *his own works*. Now he is doing the works of God.

The branch places itself at the disposal of the vine, for the vine to do with as it pleases. And we do the same, saying, 'Lord, here is my life. It's yours to do with as you please. I am available.'

There was a time in my Christian walk (and probably in yours, too) when I would come to the end of the day wondering if I had done enough for the Lord. Could I have done more? Should I have done more? How much was enough, anyway? And the Accuser would add fuel to my self-condemnation by reminding me of the many things I had left undone. Consequently, much of my at-the-close-of-the-day praying went something like this: 'Lord, forgive me. I know I didn't do all I should today. Help me do more tomorrow.'

But that was before I talked with the kitchen tap. One day, walking through the kitchen, I happened to notice that the tap seemed down in the dumps. I stopped and said, 'Hey, tap, what's the matter with you? You look discouraged.'

'Yes, master, I am.'

'Why? What happened?'

The tap looked down. 'Nothing happened – that's what happened, nothing. I failed you today. I'm sorry.'

'Failed me? How?'

'Well, Sir, I've seen you pass by a dozen times today and I haven't done anything for you. I haven't washed your hands; I haven't quenched your thirst; I haven't done anything. Oh, a couple of times I tried to turn myself on, but I was only able to squeeze out a couple of drops. It didn't amount to much. I'm sorry.'

I patted tap on the head. 'You silly tap. You're right, I have passed by you a dozen times today, and, you're right, you haven't done anything for me. You haven't turned on once today. But that's my business. If I had wanted you on I would have turned you on. If I had wanted you to wash my hands or quench my thirst, I would have turned you on. I don't want you turning yourself on – all you'll do is waste water and make a mess.'

I looked him straight in the nozzle. 'Listen to me, tap. Every time I walked by today, I knew you were here. I knew that if I wanted to use you, all I had to do was touch you and you would respond. I don't judge your faithfulness by how much water you dispense in a day. I judge you by your *availability*. And you have been faithful to me today, tap, because you have been available to me. I'm proud of you.'

I don't know if that little talk helped the tap or not, but it did me a lot of good. It reminded me that God does not judge me by the achievement of my hand, but by the ambition of my heart. As God said to David, I believe he says to us: 'You did well in that it was in your heart' (2 Chronicles 6:8).

Remember the beautiful picture Christ gave us in the Gospel of John? 'If any man is thirsty, let him come to me and drink . . . From his innermost being shall flow rivers of living water' (John 7:37,38 NAS). *You provide the riverbed and I will provide the river*. That's availability.

His Words Abiding in Us

'If my words abide in you,' said Jesus. The word *abide* is a strong one and means 'to settle down permanently, to be at home in.' Jesus means that his words must have a permanent dwelling place in our lives. Our hearts are to be a home for the word of God. We make our heart into a home when we allow his words to *control* us.

103

One of the charges God brought against his people through the prophet Hosea was that they had treated his word as a stranger (Hosea 8:12). The stranger was not at home in Israel, he had no permanent dwelling place there. He was allowed to live there but he had no voice in the land. Being a stranger, he had no 'say-so' in the affairs of Israel. He possessed no vote. Whatever opinion he might have about important decisions was ignored. God said, 'you have treated my word as a stranger.' It has no voice in daily affairs, it casts no vote. When important decisions are made, the word of God is ignored.

It's easy for our religion to become just a matter of words. We take the Bible literally, but not seriously; we're orthodox but not always obedient. The apostle John said, 'Now by this we know that we know him, if we keep his commandments. He who says, "I know him," and does not keep his commandments, is a liar, and the truth is not in him' (1 John 2:3,4).

John uses the phrase, 'He who says', over and over, as if he had a particular person in mind, perhaps someone who professed to know Jesus, but whose life denied it. These are hard words: if someone says he knows Jesus but does not keep his commandments, he is a liar. Full stop. This sounds like sinless perfection, but it isn't. No one, not even John, lives a faultless life. By that measure we're all hypocrites.

The key to understanding these verses is the word, 'keep', which means to be vigilant, to keep a watchful eye on something. It was used of ancient seamen who sailed by the stars. They kept a watchful, vigilant eye on the stars and sailed accordingly.

It took me three trips to England before I got up enough nerve to drive a car. A friend loaned us his for two weeks – if he was willing to take the risk, so was I. Some of the road signs in England are different from those in the United States – for instance, 'No Waiting on the Verge', is England's way of saying, 'No Curbside

Parking'. We bought a book that paralleled the English signs and the American signs; my wife navigated. With the book open in her lap, Kaye translated the signs and kept saying, 'Think left, think left.'

I've never been more vigilant. I kept a watchful eye on the signs and regulated my driving accordingly. That's what John is saying. A person who really knows Jesus does not have a nonchalant attitude towards his commandments.

Keeping his commandments means we have a God-reference to life. God and his word are taken into account; we bring everything under the judgment of God's word. We do not make decisions without taking into account what is pleasing to God; he is our frame of reference.

The life that prays is the life in which 'the word of Christ dwells in [us] richly' (Colossians 3:16).

Not only do the words of Christ control us, they also *cleanse* us.

'I am the true vine,' said Jesus, 'and my Father is the vinedresser. Every branch in me that does not bear fruit he takes away; and every branch that bears fruit he prunes, that it may bear more fruit' (John 15:1,2).

Earlier I mentioned the progression of fruitfulness in this passage. In verse 2 the branch *bears* fruit, then bears *more* fruit, and in verse 5, bears *much* fruit. The life that prays is not static; it is dynamic, living, growing, increasing. How does God, the Vinedresser, bring us from simply bearing fruit to bearing much fruit? Not by adding branches, but by making the branches healthier. And the branches are made healthier by pruning.

If you have watched someone prune a tree or a vine, you know that the vinedresser is merciless in his cutting. The pruning is ruthless – we would never guess that what appears to be cruelty on the part of the vinedresser, is really tenderness.

Sometimes we misjudge the Vinedresser. We may be resting in our appointed place, abiding in the vine, bearing good fruit, when suddenly heavy steps are heard entering the vineyard. Instantly the word comes through the grapevine: the Vinedresser has come, and he's carrying pruning shears. And then he's standing in front of you, and for no reason at all, he starts clipping away some of your best branches. Nearby vines try to encourage you; it will be all right, they say. You'll live through it, they say. But you know you won't. You can't understand the cruelty of the vinedresser – this, after winning the 'Most Fruitful Branch of the Year' award.

But if you're a branch, pruning is an occupational hazard. Branches are instruments, not ornaments. The word here translated 'pruning' is the word 'cleanse', which when used in reference to the vine means, 'to prune by the removal of superfluous wood'.

The Father does the pruning and the word of God is his shears (John 15:3). Everything in the branch that diverts the vital power from producing fruit is cut away. He prunes all that is bad and much that is good. Cutting off that which is bad, the most immature branch can understand, but cutting away so many good branches seems reckless and wasteful, as though the Vinedresser enjoyed pruning, enjoyed our pain. It's almost a crime – those beautiful branches, those lovely leaves, all going to waste.

But the Lord of the vineyard is only cutting away useless wood. It may be beautiful wood but it takes up room and burns precious fuel, fuel that in another branch would produce luscious grapes. We become like the thorny ground Jesus speaks of in the parable of the sower. Some seed 'fell among thorns, and the thorns sprang up and choked them' (Matthew 13:7). Later, in verse 22, Jesus explained the picture: 'Now he who received seed among the thorns is he who hears the word, and the cares of this world and the deceitfulness of riches choke the word, and he becomes unfruitful.'

We don't have to be great backsliders to become unfruitful; we get ourselves entangled in so many 'good'

106

activities. The greatest threat to the best is not the bad, but the good – good things that clutter our life so there is no room for the seed to grow, things that drain so much of our energy there is none left for bearing fruit. There is too much wood: reduce the wood and you increase the fruit.

This is graphically illustrated by an incident in the lives of Mary and Martha (Luke 10:38–42). Practically every time you see Martha, she's in the kitchen; that girl loved to cook. But she could never get Mary, her younger sister, to help her. Mary had other interests.

> Now it happened as they went that he entered a certain village; and a certain woman named Martha welcomed him into her house. And she had a sister called Mary, who also sat at Jesus' feet and heard his word. But Martha was distracted with much serving, and she approached him and said, 'Lord, do you not care that my sister has left me to serve alone? Therefore tell her to help me.'

At this point, whose side are you on? Myself, I side with Martha. It's not fair that she has to do everything by herself. Mary's just lazy. Now we'll listen to Jesus' opinion.

> And Jesus answered and said to her, 'Martha, Martha, you are worried and troubled about many things. But one thing is needed, and Mary has chosen that good part, which will not be taken away from her.'

That's a surprise. Just *one* thing needed? Are we ready for this – that out of the many things we do, good things, important things, hundreds of things, only one is needed. Yes, there is just one thing needed. Martha was so distracted by her busyness she didn't realise it. Jesus contrasted Martha's 'many things' with Mary's 'one thing'. Martha was so busy serving the Lord she had no time to enjoy his presence.

Martha's service to Christ should have brought joy and peace to her heart, but instead it brought anxiety, worry and anger. Her well-intended labour succeeded only in breaking the harmony between her and her sister, and cast a cloud of gloom over the entire affair. Does that sound familiar?

There is only one thing needed because Jesus will survive if Martha doesn't feed him *but Martha won't survive if Jesus doesn't feed her*. I've seen many successful Christians 'die on the vine' because they were so busy serving Christ they had no time to sit at his table and feast on his bread.

Poor Martha was scurrying back and forth trying to prepare a table for Jesus, when he had already spread his own table. And Mary was at her Lord's table, sitting at his feet, the pose of a receptive mind and a devoted spirit, feasting on communion with him.

And Mary had 'chosen that good part'. That is a culinary term, the parlance of the kitchen. It was the choice piece, the portion reserved for the guest of honour at the feast. While Martha thought she was preparing the choice portion for Jesus, he gave it to Mary.

In the same manner, the Vinedresser knows that only one thing is needed – not more wood but healthier wood – and so he cuts and clips that he may give the 'good portion'.

The branch probably doesn't understand any better than we do why the cutting and the hacking is necessary. It's hard to believe that this ordeal will make us more fruitful. Nonetheless, it's true. To live a life that can pray, a life that can intercede for others, a life that can identify with their cry and bear their burden, requires some experience at the hand of the Vinedresser.

What pruning is to the branch, sifting was to Peter. Jesus had a good reason for permitting Satan to sift the disciple, a reason Peter could not appreciate even if he had known what it was. Jesus said, '. . . And when you have returned to me, *strengthen your brethren*' (Luke 22:32, emphasis added). We may forget that the branch bears fruit *for others*, not for itself. The fruit, the pruning, everything, is for others.

A doctoral student from a nearby seminary came one day to interview me as a part of his class assignment. 'I'm supposed to interview seven pastors and ask them what they consider to be their primary responsibility as a minister. Could you tell me what you feel is yours?'

'I'll be glad to,' I said. 'As a pastor, my primary responsibility is me.' Before he had a chance to reply, I went on. 'My primary responsibility is to make certain every day that the rivers of living water are flowing out of my life. My people are ministered to by the overflow of my life. If there is no overflow there is no ministry. It is the Christ in me that reaches out and touches people.'

We may call it pruning, sifting or chastening, but whatever we call it, we may rest assured that it will happen. The Vinedresser knows when we need pruning and where it is needed. He will do whatever pruning it takes to make us 'bear much fruit'. And that is the life that can pray.

8: How God Answers Prayer

Zacharias was surprised when God answered his prayer.
I was surprised when God didn't answer mine.
I liked Zacharias' surprise better.

When God did not answer two of the biggest prayers of my life I was surprised because I *knew* God would answer them. He had given my wife and I a promise; we had a 'word' from God. And we had done everything we were supposed to – we had filled in all the blanks. We were as right with God as we knew how to be, we believed and prayed, we confessed and claimed, we beseeched the Lord and rebuked the devil, and we thanked God in advance for the answers. We even fasted. God had answered plenty of prayers like that before.

And I have to admit that after that disappointment prayer became very difficult for me. It seemed that every time I tried to pray, those two unanswered prayers hovered over me like two grinning demons clacking, 'What's this! Are you praying again? Remember last time.' I think I felt like C. S. Lewis must have felt when he wrote

Meanwhile, where is God? This is one of the most disquieting symptoms. When you are happy, so happy that you have no sense of needing Him, if you turn to Him with praise, you will be welcomed with open arms. But go to Him when your need is desperate, when all other help is vain and what do you find? A door slammed in your face, and a sound of bolting and double bolting on the inside. After that, silence. You may as well turn away.[1]

But I learned that this was ignorance on my part, not indifference on God's. God is bigger than our theology; our concept of prayer does not bind him. God makes no terms, gives no promises that paralyse his sovereignty. Any interpretation or application of scripture that does not leave God sovereign is a wrong interpretation. My expectations do not bind him; my wish is not his command.

God is free to act as he chooses. Take for example, the scripture that is the text for this book: Ezekiel 22:30: 'So I sought for a man among them who would make a wall, and stand in the gap before me on behalf of the land, that I should not destroy it; but I found no one.' The result? 'Therefore I have poured out my indignation on them' (verse 31). Because there was no intercessor. God poured out his wrath.

But in Isaiah 59:16, we read, 'He saw that there was no man, and wondered that there was no intercessor . . .' (verse 16a). Again, God looks for an intercessor, a man to stand in the gap, but finds none. The result? 'Therefore his own arm brought salvation for him; and his own righteousness, it sustained him' (verse 16b). Because there was no intercessor God brought forth his salvation. In Ezekiel, finding no man gave God the opportunity to show his power in judgment. In Isaiah, finding no man gave God the opportunity to show his power in salvation.

If we believe that all roses are red and someone brings us a yellow rose, we'll say it's fake because all roses are red. And here is where we get into trouble; we have a bad habit of anticipating God, of forming a mental image of God answering our prayer, with time, place and method included. We can see it – it's obvious. There's only one way our prayer can be answered; there's only one way our problem can be solved. Anybody can see that.

111

But I can't recall many times when God worked exactly as I expected. He has a way of taking the obvious and reversing it. Sometimes the answer is so unlike the picture I think God has not answered at all. The Jewish nation did something like that with Jesus. He did not look like they thought the Messiah should look, so they concluded he was not the Messiah.

To this day the ways of God in answering prayer remain a mystery to me. Which is as it should be – who would worship a God they could understand?

But I find myself in excellent company. Some mighty good people carry in their hearts divine surprises: surprise answers and surprise non-answers. Two who helped me a lot are Zacharias and Elizabeth, the parents of John the Baptist. Since Zacharias had better success with his prayer than I had with mine, it makes more sense to talk about his.

Luke introduces us to this couple in the first chapter of his Gospel as 'a certain priest named Zacharias' and his wife Elizabeth, both of whom were righteous and blameless in the sight of God. 'But they had no child, because Elizabeth was barren, and they were both well advanced in years' (Luke 1:5-7).

One day while Zacharias was burning incense in the temple, an angel appeared and said, 'Do not be afraid, Zacharias, for your prayer is heard; and your wife Elizabeth will bear you a son, and you shall call his name John' (verses 11-13).

Then Zacharias asked a phenomenal question: 'How shall I know this? For I am an old man, and my wife is well advanced in year?' (verse 18). I call that a phenomenal question because if an angel suddenly appeared before me and told me my prayer was answered, I would tend to believe him. But even the personal appearance of an angel with a special delivery message did not convince Zacharias. And this was no post-office clerk – this was Gabriel, 'who stands in the presence of God' (verse 19), and he struck Zacharias dumb becausehe did not believe the angel's words. If God dealt with unbelief that way today, most of us would spend the rest of our lives speechless.

But Zacharias had a good reason for asking his question. Years of unanswered prayer had made him slow to believe. This prayer Gabriel was referring to, their prayer for a child, must have been close to prehistoric, for they were both well past the age of childbearing. By the way, doesn't Zacharias phrase it beautifully? 'How shall I know this? For I am an old man, and my wife is well advanced in years' (verse 18). He didn't say, 'I'm an old man and my wife is an old woman'; He said, 'My wife is well advanced in years.' The old King James says it best: 'My wife is *well-stricken* in years.' Zacharias was as delicate as a diplomat.

But we must not be too hard on him for doubting the angel's words. His dream of being a father had long since surrendered to reality. And yet . . .

And yet here was an angel straight from God, avowing it was going to happen. Zacharias began to learn some things about the way God answers prayer.

Answered Later

When does God answer prayer? He always answers immediately but sometimes later. I'm not trying to be clever. When we offer an 'answerable' prayer, that is, one that is according to his will (1 John 5:14, 15), he hears and answers immediately. The Lord doesn't convene a committee to examine the facts and advise and consent. Nor does he need time to consider the request. 'It shall come to pass, that before they call, I will answer; and while they are still speaking, I will hear' (Isaiah 65:24).

The *granting* of the prayer is immediate, but the *giving* of it into our hands may be delayed.

This is what the angel was trying to tell Zacharias:

113

'Your prayer is heard' (verse 13). The wording makes it appear that Zacharias had been praying for a son even as he ministered in the temple that day. But the fact is, they had long since given up on that prayer; Zacharias' question to the angel shows that. A child was a discarded hope.* Now we can understand his question.

But there is another clue to the answer to this prayer. The phrase, 'Your prayer is heard' is important. The tense of the Greek word translated 'heard' can be expressed, *'was heard'*, and in keeping with the context, it should be. This was a prayer that had been offered in the past – and *answered* in the past.

In the Greek text, 'heard', has a prefix attached to it, making it a rare word, occurring only five times in the New Testament. The prefix expresses purpose, action, tendency, result. With the prefix and verb joined, a literal translation is, 'Your prayer was *heard-to-do*.' When God heard their prayer, he also *did* it. God had granted their request years before, perhaps, and now he was going to *give* it.

We see this same idea in Daniel chapter 10. The prophet had prayed and fasted for three weeks without receiving an answer of any kind. Then an angel appeared with this message:

> Do not fear, Daniel: for from the *first day* that you set your heart to understand, and to humble yourself before your God, your words were heard; and I have come because of your words.

---

* Some interpreters hold that Zacharias' prayer would not be in keeping with Zacharias' presence at the altar. A prayer for personal blessing would be unthinkable and unworthy of his position; 'his prayer for a son was actually a prayer for the salvation of the people or for the promised Messiah'. But this is a strained interpretation and ignores the context and the personal pronouns, i.e., *your* wife shall bear *you* a son.

114

But the prince of the kingdom of Persia withstood me twenty-one days; and behold, Michael, one of the chief princes, came to help me, for I had been left alone there with the kings of Persia' (Daniel 10:12, 13 emphasis added).

This isn't the place to clear all the cobwebs out of those words – what is significant for our purpose is the fact that Daniel prayed and fasted for three weeks, and twenty-one days later an angel arrived with an answer and an explanation. Daniel's prayers had been heard the first day he had uttered them, and on that first day the angel had been dispatched with an answer, but he had been held up in heavy traffic for twenty-one days.

'From the first day . . . your words were heard.' The *granting* was immediate but the *giving* was delayed.

We are familiar with this prayer promise: 'Therefore I say to you, whatever things you ask when you pray, believe that you receive them, and you will have them' (Mark 11:24). The New English Bible reads, 'I tell you, then, whatever you ask for in prayer, believe that you *have received it* and *it will be yours*' (emphasis added).

The Williams translation highlights the sense of the Greek tenses: 'So then I tell you, whenever your pray and ask for anything have faith that it *has been granted* you, and you *will get it*' (Emphasis added).

It doesn't take much faith to believe you have something when you already have it. But to believe that you have something when you don't have it – that's faith.

'Believe that you have it and you will get it,' Jesus says. Believe you've already got it and you'll get it. The *granting* is immediate, but the *giving* of it into your hands may be delayed.

Answered Better

Zacharias also learned that God often answers later in order to answer better.

On my desk is a pencil holder with this motto: 'God always gives the best to those who leave the choice with him.' Is that true?

I think some people believe the Bible because they don't know what it says. For example, the Bible says in Psalm 34:10 that 'those who seek the Lord shall not lack any good thing.' And in Psalm 84:11 it makes this promise: 'No good thing will he withhold from those who walk uprightly.' Do we really believe that? Then why do we complain when he withholds something from us? If it had been a good thing for us, he would have given it to us. Ruth Graham, the wife of Billy Graham, is quoted as saying, 'If God had answered every prayer of mine, I would have married the wrong man seven times.' Thank God for some unanswered prayers.

God not only answers later, he answers better. Suppose God had given Zacharias and Elizabeth a son in their younger years, when they first asked for one? To be sure, they would have been thrilled and they would have loved him with all their hearts. But in the final analysis, he would have been just another boy who had been born, had lived his life and died, a handful of unremembered dust. No one would remember him today; no sermons would be preached about him; his name, and the names of his parents, would not have been immortalised in the Scriptures.

But God gave them something better. He gave them John the Baptist, the last Old Testament prophet, the only Old Testament prophet who lived to see his prophecy fulfilled, the first cousin of Jesus Christ, the forerunner of the Messiah, the man of whom Jesus said of those born of woman, none was greater than he.

There's a good chance, of course, that, at the time, Zacharias and Elizabeth would not have agreed. Probably, they didn't think that it was better to wait until they were old. *But we know better*.

And he gave them the unexpected joy of a son in their old age, a joy rarely experienced by couples their age, a joy multiplied by the long years of waiting. As their years declined, their joy soared. God saved the best wine till last.

When the Situation Becomes Humanly Impossible

Zacharias discovered that God often waits until the situation is humanly impossible.

A strange thing happened shortly after our church started its intercessory prayer ministry. One Sunday morning at the conclusion of the worship service, a young woman with a pained look on her face, drew me aside and began whispering to me. She was one of several women in our church whose husbands were unsaved and had enlisted in the new prayer ministry with high hopes. That had been three months ago.

'There's something wrong,' she whispered.

'What is it?'

'My husband,' she said. 'I've been praying for him for three months and . . .'

'And?'

Tears came to her eyes; she was trying hard not to cry. 'He's worse than ever,' she blurted out. 'He's more hostile toward God, toward the church – toward me. It's not getting better – it's getting worse.'

I had received similar reports from others. A man had come to my study several months back and we had covenanted together to pray about a serious financial problem in his business. Later, when I asked him how things were going, he shook his head and said, 'Terrible.' Putting his hand on my shoulder, he said jokingly (I think), 'You know, preacher, sometimes I wish you had never got me into this praying business.'

But this is one of God's ways: he often allows a situation to deteriorate before he intervenes. With Zacharias and Elizabeth he waited until both were well past the age of childbearing. When it became physically impossible

117

for them to have children, God gave them a son.

This means that some things may get worse before they get better. I caution would-be intercessors not to be surprised if something like this occurs, as though some strange thing happened to them. I have watched people for whom I was praying gradually shift from indifference to hostility. That, I believe, may be a symptom of the Spirit's convicting activity. When God closes in on an individual that person cannot remain indifferent – and you can also expect the Enemy to mount a counterattack to recapture lost ground.

In other words, I have discovered that whatever I am praying about – *on its way to better, it may become worse for a while*.

God worked this way with Abraham and Sarah. He promised Abraham he would be a father of many nations, that all nations of the earth would be blessed through his seed, a seed so vast it would be easier to count the number of stars in heaven than to number the issue of his seed. And Abraham 'believed in the Lord' (Genesis 15:16).

But it's hard to keep believing when old age catches up with you and nothing has happened. So hard to believe, in fact, you run in a replacement, Ishmael. But God waited until Abraham was one hundred years old and Sarah ninety years old before he *gave* what he had already *granted*.

Even when God renewed the promise (Genesis 17), Abraham found it hard to believe. He 'laughed, and said in his heart, "Shall a child be born to a man who is one hundred years old? And shall Sarah, who is ninety years old, bear a child?"' (Genesis 17:17). Abraham laughed. He couldn't help himself – the idea was ridiculous. He laughed because he didn't believe.

And we know Sarah didn't believe it, either, because she laughed too. If a ninety-year-old woman discovers she's pregnant, there are any number of things she might do – but laughing is not one of them.

Why does God work this way?

God always takes the route that brings him the greatest glory. I believe we can file that under 'Heaven's Fixed Laws'. As we saw in Chapter Two, the motive behind our asking and the motive behind his answering is 'that the Father may be glorified in the Son' (John 14:13). The farther back we track these things, the more we will see that everything leads to this destination: the glory of God. Abraham was 'strengthened in faith, giving glory to God' (Romans 4:20). When bearing children was no longer possible, when Abraham could no longer take matters into his own hands (as he had done in the case of Ishmael) God moved. And when finally the child was born, there was no doubt that God had done it – he received the credit and the glory.

Because we don't understand this, God seems at times to stand idly by while we sink beneath the waves. Hurt and outraged by his apathy, we cry, 'Master carest thou not that we perish?' But that is *our* opinion. We are not perishing and he is not unconcerned.

I remember the first time I heard Manley Beasley speak. It was an informal gathering, not more than fifty or sixty people, ministers and their wives, mostly. Manley, an evangelist and revivalist, was recovering from a two-year bout with five diseases, three of which were terminal – at least, they were supposed to be. Only days out of the hospital and too weak to stand, he sat on a high stool and, in obvious pain, spoke in a soft voice. His opening words were: 'Folks, God won't hurt you.'

At the time, God was killing me.

But that was my opinion. God was not killing me; he was saving me (I remembered reading something about 'losing your life to save it'). Like Moses, I wanted to see the face of God; I wanted to see him from the front; I wanted a glance at the script. Before I followed him I wanted to know where he was going.

But, like Moses, I travel under sealed orders. I see God

119

only in retrospect. When I pause and look back at the way I've come, I see the hand of God at every turn and know that the 'Saviour has led each step of the way.'

This fact, perhaps more than any other, has cushioned me in rough times when answers were long in coming. It is a buffer that keeps the sharp edges of life from severing the jugular.

Remember: *God takes the route that brings him the most glory.* And: *on its way to better, it may become worse for a while.*

Linked to Divine Necessity

Zacharias also learned that God answers prayer when it is linked to divine necessity.

I realise God has no 'needs' and no 'problems', but I want to use these words to illustrate this point. Why did God choose that particular time to answer Zacharias' prayer? Why not ten years earlier? Why not ten years later? I believe God answered when he did because he 'needed' to answer then. The fullness of time had come, and he 'needed' John the Baptist. God 'needed' the forerunner of the Messiah, and in meeting Zacharias' need, he met his own. By solving Zacharias' problem, he solved his own 'problem'.

And then there is Hannah. Her story is told in 1 Samuel Chapter 1. In her struggle with the stigma of barrenness, she personifies the reproach endured by all the childless women of the Bible. Year after year Hannah cried before the Lord, begging him to remove her disgrace and give her a son. Her burden was so great she could not express it in words; she groaned her supplication to God, moving her lips but uttering no sound. When Eli, the priest, saw her in the temple praying with such emotion, he accused her of being drunk.

But the Lord answered her prayer – finally. He gave her a son whom she gave back to the Lord, a son called Samuel who became the great judge and prophet of Israel.

When did God answer her prayer? When he 'needed' to. There came a time when God 'needed' Samuel, when Israel 'needed' a judge and a prophet, and in solving Hannah's 'problem', he solved his own.

God always moves with redemptive purpose. Jesus performed many miracles – but not a one for show. I remember as a boy sitting in the balcony of the old Temple Theatre, seeing for the first time the original (and silent) black-and-white classic, *The King of Kings*. I watched the soldiers drag Jesus before Herod. And when Herod demanded Jesus work a miracle, I leaned forward in my seat to urge Jesus on – if Herod saw a miracle, he would let Jesus go. I knew how the story ended, but I got caught up in the drama. I couldn't believe that Jesus would just stand there and not even speak to Herod; all he had to do was work one little miracle and he would have gone free.

Why didn't he? He could have – and that seemed a mighty good time to do one. Besides, weren't the miracles intended as signs of his Messiahship? Why didn't he dazzle old Herod with one?

That kind of miracle was pre-empted by the redemptive purpose of God. Jesus confined his miracles to that realm. When Jesus stood silent before Herod, he knew his hour had come, the hour he spoke of in John 12:27. He did not want to escape from Herod and his soldiers, or from Pilate, or from the Jewish leaders and their mobs – he had come to die.

Our prayers must be linked to divine necessity; they must flow in the stream of God's redemptive activity. This is another way of saying that we must pray according to the will of God.

'According to the will of God', is another intimidating phrase in the Christian vocabulary. This, perhaps, more than any other one thing, discourages Christians from praying with confidence. It's scary to think that we might miss God's will and spend the rest of our life paying for it.

But we cannot know the will of God about every detail of our lives. And we do not need to know the will of God about everything we pray for. That is, the *immediate* will of God. But we can know the *ultimate* will of God. For example, I may be out of a job and unable to provide for my family. I can pray with assurance for my needs to be met because God has promised to supply all my needs (Philippians 4:19). That is what I would call the *ultimate* will of God. The *immediate* will of God has to do with *how* God meets that need. I know that when I ask God to meet my needs I am praying according to the will of God. But I may not have that same assurance if I ask God to meet my needs by winning a million dollars in the Publishers' Clearing House Contest. Having my needs met is the *ultimate* will of God. Winning the million dollars is the *immediate* will of God. I know God will supply my needs, but he may not do it by making me a millionaire. I know he won't. I've asked.

What To Say
When You Don't Know What To Say

There is a way to know that we are praying 'according to his will'. In his last public discourse, as he drew within sight of the cross, Jesus laid bare his distress: 'Now my soul is troubled, and what shall I say? Father, save me from this hour? But for this purpose I came to this hour. *Father, glorify your name*' (John 12:27, 28, emphasis added).

'Troubled' in the depth of his being, Jesus debated within himself: 'What shall I say?' He could ask his Father to save him from the cross. But this 'hour' was the reason he came into the world. This is a remarkable drawing aside of the mystery of the God-man to allow us a glimpse of the humanness of Jesus. 'What shall I say?' Would we have ever dreamed that the Son of God could be at a loss for words, so deeply divided within himself that he would cry, 'What shall I say?'

He settled the conflict with these words: 'Father, glorify your name.' That's what to say when you don't know what to say. That's what to pray when you don't know what to pray. It is always right to say, 'Father, glorify your name.' When we throw that blanket over our petitions, we are praying in the will of God.

To me, this means that the glory of God, the honour of his name, outranks all petitions; it means that if I have to choose (assuming I had the right to choose) between God being glorified and my petition being granted, I would choose the glory of God.

One Friday afternoon when I was in college, a friend and I decided to drive home for the weekend. We piled into my 1946 Ford and, both of us being ministerial students, I asked my friend to pray for a safe trip. I bowed my head, closed my eyes and heard him say, 'Dear Lord, we pray that you will protect us and give us travelling mercies – unless we can glorify thee better on a hospital bed.'

If memory serves, that was the last time I asked him to pray.

In a crazy kind of way, my friend was right. Whatever we pray for, it is a given that the glory of God takes precedence. Sometimes God withholds the lesser in order to give the greater, and it may be that he cannot give me what I want without compromising his own plan. This is praying as Jesus prayed, 'Father, if it is your will, remove this from me; nevertheless, not my will, but yours, be done' (Luke 22:42).

How Long?

I am frequently asked how long we should pray for something. If God delays the answer of a prayer as he did with Zacharias, how can we know if it's a delay or a denial? We don't want to keep asking for something God has said no to. On the other hand, we don't want to give up asking if he is telling us to wait.

I suggest we pray and keep on praying until one of three things happens.

1. *Pray and keep on praying until we receive the answer.* Some say it is a lack of faith to ask more than once, that it is an act of unbelief that voids our prayer. The argument runs like this: at four o'clock a boy asks his father to take him to the park the next day; the father says, yes, he will. At five o'clock the boy asks again, and again the father says that he will. At six o'clock the boy asks again, and again at seven o'clock, and again at eight. Why does the boy keep asking? He doesn't believe his father. Thus, if we truly have faith, we need ask only once.

I admit that sounds reasonable (and it has merit) but I'm not sure it's scriptural. Jesus emphasised persistence in prayer: the only two parables he gave about prayer both emphasise persistence (The Friend at Midnight, Luke 11, and the Woman and the Judge, Luke 18). In Matthew 7:7–11 Jesus tells us to ask, to seek and to find; the tenses of the verbs say, ask and keep on asking, seek and keep on seeking, knock and keep on knocking. So, ask and keep on asking until we receive.

2. *Pray and keep on praying until we have the assurance that we will receive it.* In the early days of our church prayer ministry, a group of women met each week to pray. It happened that they all went to the same hairdresser, who was not a Christian. They prayed for her for weeks and weeks, until one day when they came together to pray, they couldn't pray for the girl's salvation. Instead, they found themselves thanking God for her salvation; a peace had settled in their hearts about the whole matter. Later one of the women said she actually felt guilty because she had lost her burden for the girl and no longer prayed for her salvation. About three weeks later in the Sunday morning service the hairdresser came to Christ. Everybody was surprised except the women who had prayed for her.

Sometimes when we are praying for something, there will come a quiet assurance that God has heard and answered. Where there was a burden now there is peace.

3. *Pray and keep on praying until God says no.* Either by spiritual intuition, light from his Word, changed circumstances, or in some other way, God may say no to us. By spiritual intuition, I mean that when God says no to a request, we have no peace in praying for it, it doesn't feel right, there is a sense of restraint.

God is more anxious for us to know his will than we are. For many finding God's will is a game of hide-and-seek, like hunting for green Easter eggs in tall grass. When someone asks me, how do I find God's will? my answer is, you don't. God's will finds you. It is not your responsibility to *find* God's will. If God wants you to know his will, it is his responsibility to reveal it.

Suppose I tell my daughter, Kimberly, that I want her to do something for me. She says she will and asks me what it is.

'I'm not going to tell you,' I say. 'You have to guess at it. And if you guess wrong, you're in trouble.'

Ridiculous, isn't it? If I have a task for my child, it is my responsibility to reveal it; her responsibility is to hear and obey.

In Romans 12:1, 2, Paul tells us that we can prove what the will of God is; we can look at two choices and discern which one is God's will. But first, he tells us to present ourselves to God, 'present' meaning *to submit*, or *to yield*.

Basically, Paul is saying that if we want to know God's will we should accept it before we know it. The 'tell me what it is and I'll decide' stance never prevails with God. Knowing that God's will, whatever it is, is always best, I submit to it before I know what it is. I accept God's will in advance.

How Will We Know?

Have you ever wished you had a spiritual referee around to tell you when you step out of bounds? Well, that's exactly what we have. Listen to Colossians 3:15: 'And let the peace of God rule in your hearts, to which also you were called in one body; and be thankful.' *Rule* is the translation of a Greek word that means 'to act as umpire'. The Williams translation makes it clear; 'Let the peace that Christ can give keep on *acting as umpire* in your hearts' (emphasis added).

The Beck translation reads, 'Let the peace of Christ . . . be in your hearts *to decide things* for you' (emphasis added).

Through Christ, the Christian has two kinds of peace, peace *with* God and the peace *of* God. Peace with God is the result of being justified by faith (Romans 5:1). The war between God and the Christian is over and he has been brought into a right relationship with God, a place of blessing. Peace with God is objective. Every believer possesses this regardless of his spiritual status. Nothing can disturb our peace with God.

Then there is the peace *of* God. This is God's peace, the peace that he himself enjoys and shares with us. This peace is subjective, an inner calm and quiet assurance of the heart. The peace of God is the believer's heart at rest. Stepping outside the will of God disturbs this peace; our heart becomes troubled, the quiet assurance disappears.

Paul is saying that we are to let the peace of Christ be the umpire in our lives, to let it decide what is right and wrong. When we lose that inner peace, when our heart is troubled and ill at ease, our spiritual umpire is blowing the whistle and calling a foul.

At times as I pray about a particular thing, there comes, suddenly or gradually, a check on my heart, a restraint. I don't feel right about it. In other words, I don't have peace about it. I take that as the umpire calling that prayer out of bounds.

The more sensitive we become to the Holy Spirit's leading, the more we will be able to discern petitions that are and are not 'according to the will of God'.

Let me sum up all this with two statements that help me. First, I pray in the direction of my burden. I pray what is 'on my heart'. This is one of the ways God leads us and we should learn to respond to the burden of our heart, believing that God has placed it there.

Second, I pray until the burden is gone. As long as the burden is there, I keep praying. When that burden is lifted, whether because God says no or says wait, I am released from that prayer.

Disclaimer: Please Read

I have mixed feeling about writing on 'how' to pray. No one is really qualified to tell others how they should approach God in prayer. I've probably raised more questions than I have answered. There is always a 'What if . . . ?' But you can't say everything in one book. So don't worry about it. Just do it. Jump out there and pray – the Holy Spirit will catch you and take you where you need to go.

9: Fasting – The Weeping of the Soul
A Biblical Survey

When I was nine years old our family moved into a new house. On the kitchen wall right above the stove, painted in red script, was this motto: 'The Way To A Man's Heart Is Through His Stomach.' Though today some might scorn that as a sexist statement, the truth of it has been confirmed a million times over. As a matter of fact, the devil has been operating under that same motto for thousands of years. He discovered long ago that the way to a man's heart is through his physical appetites.

The first temptation hurled at man was related to his physical appetite. 'When the woman saw that the tree was good for food, she took from its fruit and ate; and she gave to her husband with her, and he ate' (Genesis 3:6).

Since that first garden experience, there has been a steady stream of temptation aimed at the appetite. After a mighty deliverance from the judgment of God, Noah abused his physical appetite and got drunk. Isaac favoured Esau above Jacob because Esau was a hunter and provided his father with plenty of good meat. Unfortunately Esau allowed his stomach to overrule his good sense and sold his birthright for a bowl of chilli.

Notice how Paul describes, in 1 Corinthians 10:7, the idolatry of Israel after their escape from Egypt. If I had been called upon to report the incident, I think I would have mentioned the golden calf and the other shenanigans that took place. Not Paul. He states it simply: 'The people sat down to eat and drink, and stood up to play.'

He knew the real issue was not the calf but the uncontrolled physical appetite.

In the wilderness temptation of Jesus, the devil aimed his first barrage at the physical appetite of the Son of Man: 'If you are the Son of God, command that these stones become bread' (Matthew 4:3). Later, Paul warned the Philippians to steer clear of people 'whose god is their appetite' (Philippians 3:19).

In these passages and many others, the Bible reveals a pronounced relationship between a person's spiritual status and his physical appetite. A lack of discipline here is symptomatic of a lack of discipline in other areas of life. Perhaps this is why the Bible has so much to say about fasting.

Many Christians are surprised to discover the prominence of fasting in the Bible. Most of us probably have never seriously considered fasting as a part of Christian living. Because we associate it with fanatical or legalistic religions, we have practically dismissed it as being relevant to twentieth-century Christianity. But no serious study of the deeper truths of intercession can afford to overlook fasting or relegate it to an unimportant status. So, a quick survey is in order.

After his encounter with Jezebel, Elijah, in desperate need of personal revival, went to Mount Horeb where he fasted for forty days (1 Kings 19:8).

Esther's fast played an important role in the deliverance she obtained for her people (Esther 4:16).

David fasted when his baby was stricken (2 Samuel 12:16). Daniel fasted and prayed until God's heavenly messenger broke through enemy lines to bring Daniel an answer from the throne of God (Daniel 10:3). Both Ezra and Nehemiah proclaimed fasts during national crises (Ezra 8:21; Nehemiah 1:4). Through the prophet Jeremiah, God commanded his people to fast regularly every year (Jeremiah 36:6,9).

But fasting is not confined to the Old Testament. In

Luke 2:37 it is recorded of Anna, the prophetess, that she 'never left the temple, serving night and day with fastings and prayers'. John the Baptist fasted and taught his disciples to do likewise.

Jesus practised fasting and made it clear that he expected his followers to do the same. Take Matthew 6, for example. Jesus warns his disciples about doing the right thing for the wrong motive. The Christian life, he says, is fragile; handle it with care. Make certain your motives are pure. To illustrate his point he takes three representative religious practices and shows how these can be performed for the praise of men rather than for the praise of God.

The three he mentions are almsgiving, prayer and fasting. Note the wording in verse 16: 'And whenever you fast . . .' Again in verse 17: 'But you, when you fast . . .' Jesus did not say, *if* you fast, but *when* you fast. It was expected that his disciples would fast. Jesus here makes fasting just as much a religious duty as almsgiving and prayer. No modern Christian would claim that almsgiving (acts of charity) and prayers are out of date. And neither is fasting. Jesus placed it on the same plane with prayer and acts of charity.

In Matthew 9:14–15, we find, 'Then the disciples of John came to him, saying, "Why do we and the Pharisees fast, but your disciples do not fast?" And Jesus said to them, "The attendants of the bridegroom cannot mourn, as long as the bridegroom is with them, can they? But the days will come when the bridegroom is taken away from them, and then they will fast."'

While Jesus was physically present with his disciples they had no need to fast. The time for fasting would come when Jesus was taken out of the world. And today as we still await the return of the bridegroom, there are times when fasting is called for.

Immediately following his conversion, the apostle Paul fasted for three days (Acts 9:9). Fasting was a permanent part of his life and ministry. When writing to the Corinthians of his own personal ministry, he says, 'But in everything commending ourselves as servants of God, in much endurance, in afflictions, in hardships, in distresses, in stripes, in imprisonments, in tumults, in labours, in watchings, in *fastings*' (2 Corinthians 6:5, emphasis added).

Then again later in 2 Corinthians 11:27: 'I have been in labour and hardship, through many sleepless nights, in hunger and thirst, often without food [Greek: fasting], in cold and exposure.'

The book of Acts shows that fasting was a vital part of the young church's life. 'And while they were ministering to the Lord and fasting, the Holy Spirit said, "Set apart Barnabas and Saul for the work to which I have called them." Then when they had fasted and prayed and laid their hands on them, they sent them away' (Acts 13:2–3 RSV).

Acts 14:23 describes the missionary ministry of Paul and Barnabas in strengthening the newly formed congregations. 'And when they had appointed elders for them in every church, having prayed with fasting, they commended them to the Lord in whom they had believed' (RSV).

A Definition

The Hebrew word means 'to cover the mouth' and the Greek words mean simply, 'not to eat'. But fasting is much more than going hungry. As a matter of fact, fasting isn't confined to food and water, though that is its primary expression. By mutual agreement, a husband and wife may 'fast' from sexual relations in order to devote themselves fully to prayer (1 Corinthians 7:5).

Let me offer this definition: *fasting is the voluntary abstinence of satisfaction from certain physical appetites, for spiritual reasons*. Most often, fasting is abstaining from food and drink, though it could be any number of things.

Different Kinds of Fasts

The Bible speaks of different kinds of fasts. Some fasts are public. After hearing the prophetic message of Jonah, the king of Nineveh proclaimed a fast throughout the city, denying even the animals food and water (Jonah 3:5–10). The prophet Joel called for a nationwide fast for the purpose of seeking the Lord for mercy and revival (Joel 1:14).

But much of our fasting is to be *private*. In Matthew 6:16–18, Jesus warns us against dressing or behaving in a manner that would cause men to know we were fasting.

How Long Does A Fast Last?

The Bible records fasts of one day, three days, seven days, twenty-one days and forty days. There is no fixed time limit. Jesus was 'led of the Spirit' to fast for forty days (Matthew 4:1,2) and we must allow the Holy Spirit to lead us in the matter of length. Normally, a Christian who is sensitive enough to the Spirit to start a fast will be sensitive enough to know when to stop.

Degrees of Fasting

One of the most interesting features of fasting in the Bible is the varying degrees of a fast. Some went without food and water, others without food, still others abstained only from wine and pleasant bread. I think it will be helpful to categorise these differing degrees.

There is the *extreme fast* in which no food or drink is taken. Paul's fast in Acts 9:9 was an extreme fast. Moses' fast while receiving the law from God falls into this category. He went without food and drink for forty days – an extremely difficult task.

In a *normal fast* one abstains from food but drinks water. This is the usual method of fasting. Elijah's fast was probably a normal fast, for the Bible speaks only of his going without food (1 Kings 19:8). It is thought that Jesus drank water during his forty-day fast since the Gospel accounts mention only his hunger.

Then there is the *partial fast*. This is described in Daniel 10:3: 'I did not eat any tasty food, nor did meat or wine enter my mouth, nor did I use ointment at all, until the entire three weeks were completed.'

Why Fast?

Let me emphasise this important point: in the Bible, the purpose of fasting is always *spiritual*, to attain some spiritual end. While fasting can be an aid to health in purifying the body and taking off weight, this is not fasting in the biblical sense. And for me, this is true, that when I feel God leading me to fast for some reason, I have no trouble doing it. The hunger barely bothers me. But when I fast to lose weight, it is war on every front.

Fasting For Spiritual Discipline

It appears from the Scripture that God's original purpose in commanding the people to fast was for self-abasement and self-humbling. In Psalm 35:13 David says, 'But as for me, when they were sick, my clothing was sackcloth: I humbled my soul with fasting.' Again, in Psalm 69:10, he says, 'When I wept and chastened my soul with fasting, that was my reproach.' This is a beautiful thought – *fasting is the weeping of the soul*. Then in Psalm 109:24, 'My knees are weak through fasting; and my flesh faileth of fatness.'

In Ezra 8:21, we read, 'Then I proclaimed a fast there at the river Ahava, that we might humble ourselves before our God' (NAS).

One of the things God desires most from his people is self-humbling. We sometimes pray, 'Lord, make me humble.' But I don't think that's a biblical prayer. I find nowhere in the Bible where God is supposed to humble us. He may humiliate us, but we have to humble ourselves. That's our responsibility. And I repeat: self-humbling delights the heart of God and makes it possible for him to bless us. The apostle Peter declares, 'You younger men, likewise, be subject to your elders, and all of you, clothe yourselves with humility toward one another, for *God is opposed to the proud, but gives grace to the humble*. Humble yourselves, therefore, under the mighty hand of God, that he may exalt you at the proper time' (1 Peter 5:5,6 NAS, emphasis added).

Jesus' call to discipleship is a call to deny self in order that we may discover our all in him. Fasting is a perfect expression of godly sorrow and repentance because genuine sorrow overrides our desire for food. Thus, fasting becomes an outward expression of our inner repentance.

Remember the relation between physical appetite and spiritual discipline. The sin of Sodom was linked with a 'surfeit of food'. Of Israel, God said, 'When I fed them to the full, they committed adultery.' When the appetite for food and drink is abused, the life is laid open to attacks in other areas. The opposite is also true: when the physical appetites are brought under control, the spiritual life is strengthened and reinforced. I can't emphasise this too strongly. *Fasting is a spiritual discipline that helps subdue the body and master the appetite.*

Fasting As A Spiritual Companion

Fasting is rarely practised alone. It is always linked with another spiritual activity. Nowhere are we commanded to fast only, but to fast *and* pray, to put on sackcloth and ashes (signs of godly sorrow and repentance) *and* fast, to seek the Lord *with* fasting, or to minister to the Lord *with* fasting.

Fasting creates an atmosphere in which these other spiritual exercises can be done more effectively; they flourish in a fasting climate. Fasting is the perfect environment for prayer and seeking the Lord. With fasting we detach ourselves from the earth and with prayer attach ourselves to heaven. It enables us to abandon ourselves more completely to God during times of intense spiritual devotion. Along with many others, I have found that during seasons of fasting, I have more liberty in prayer, more enlightenment in Bible study and a deeper sense of God's presence.

Fasting under the Spirit's leadership heightens our spiritual understanding and makes us more sensitive to the things of God. Jesus' forty-day fast in the wilderness prepared him for the satanic onslaught he had to face. It was through prayer and fasting that Daniel received a revelation from God. As the church at Antioch was ministering to the Lord and fasting, the Holy Spirit revealed to them his plan for Paul and Barnabas. It was in an atmosphere of prayer and fasting that Paul and Barnabas appointed elders to the church and commended them to the Lord. In Deuteronomy 9:9,10, Moses tells us that he received the law in a climate of fasting and waiting.

Fasting For Divine Protection

An example of fasting for deliverance and protection is found in Ezra 8:21-23: 'Then I proclaimed a fast there at the river Ahava, that we might humble ourselves before our God *to seek from him a safe journey for us, our little ones, and all our possessions*. For I was ashamed to request from the king troops and horsemen to protect us from the enemy on the way, because we had said to the king, "The hand of our God is favourably disposed to all who seek him, but his power and his anger are against all those who forsake him." So we fasted and sought our

God concerning this matter, and he listened to our entreaty' (NAS, emphasis added).

This is a beautiful story. The people are about to begin a four-month march from Babylon to Jerusalem, a journey that will take them through a stony desert infested with bands of thieves. The king offered his soldiers to accompany Ezra and his people, but Ezra declined, boasting that their God was all the protection they needed. But it's easy to talk about trusting God when you are safely behind the walls of Babylon. It's another story when you find yourself in the midst of danger without the strong arm of the flesh to support you. And right here is where many Christians give the world cause to mock. Thank God, when the chips were down, Ezra didn't run to the world for help. He was ashamed to. Though Ezra was walking in human flesh, he did not war with the weapons of the flesh, but proclaimed a fast and sought the Lord, and the Lord delivered them.

2 Chronicles 20 records one of the strangest battles ever fought (see Chapter Four). King Jehoshaphat was facing an attack from an overwhelming Syrian army. He had enough sense to be afraid and 'turned his attention to seek the Lord; and proclaimed a fast throughout all Judah' (2 Chronicles 20:3 NAS) and then cried to the Lord, 'O our God, wilt thou not judge them? For we are powerless before this great multitude who are coming against us; nor do we know what to do, but our eyes are on thee' (verse 12). While they were fasting and praying, God gave them the battle plan. And what a plan it was – the king was to send the music makers out before the fighting troops. Those who were appointed to sing to the Lord and praise him went out before the army, 'and when they began singing and praising, the Lord set ambushes against the sons of Ammon, Moab and Mount Seir who had come against Judah; so they were routed' (verse 22).

Could it be that in our day God is waiting to reveal his battle plan that would deliver us from our enemies? Is he waiting for another Jehoshaphat to seek the Lord and proclaim a fast throughout the land?

Fasting To Avert God's Wrath

God had spoken. In forty days Nineveh would be destroyed. So certain was this judgment that when it was averted, Jonah, the prophetic proclaimer of that advancing doom, became angry with the Lord and pleaded to die. But the king of that wicked city repented in sackcloth and ashes and declared a fast in the city. And the Bible says, 'When God saw their deeds, that they turned from their wicked ways, then God relented concerning the calamity which he had declared he would bring upon them. And he did not do it' (Jonah 3:10 NAS).

Everywhere I go I find Christians longing for another Great Awakening to sweep across the country, a moving of the Spirit of God that will breathe new life into dead churches, Christianise atheistic schools and bind up broken homes. Scores of recipes and prescriptions for revival are offered, but you can't improve upon the 'recipe' found in the book of Joel. The Lord said:

Consecrate a fast,
Proclaim a solemn assembly;
Gather the elders
And all the inhabitants of the land
To the house of the Lord your God,
And cry out to the Lord.
'Yet even now,' declares the Lord,
Return to me with all your heart,
And with fasting, weeping and mourning . . .
Blow a trumpet in Zion,
Consecrate a fast, proclaim a solemn assembly (Joel 1:14;2:12,15 NAS).

Joel goes on to say that everyone is to take part in this – even the bride and groom are to postpone their wedding and to pray and fast until revival comes. And come it will, for God promises that in response to their prayer and fasting, he will

be zealous for his land,
And will have pity on his people.
And the Lord will answer and say to his people,
'Behold, I am going to send you grain, new wine, and oil,
And you will be satisfied in full with them;
And I will never again make you a reproach among the nations.
But I will remove the northern army far from you,
And I will drive it into a parched and desolate land,
And its vanguard into the eastern sea,
And its rear guard into the western sea.
And its stench will arise and its foul smell will come up,
For it has done great things.'
Do not fear, O land, rejoice and be glad,
For the Lord has done great things.
Do not fear, beasts of the field,
For the pastures of the wilderness have turned green,
For the tree has borne its fruit,
The fig tree and the vine have yielded in full.
So rejoice, O sons of Zion,
And be glad in the Lord your God;
For he has given you the early rain as before.
And the threshing floors will be full of grain,
And the vats will overflow with the new wine and oil.
Then I will make up to you for the years
That the swarming locust has eaten,
The creeping locust, the stripping locust, and the gnawing locust,
My great army which I sent among you.

And you shall have plenty to eat and be satisfied,
And praise the name of the Lord your God,
Who has dealt wondrously with you;
Then my people will never be put to shame.
Thus you will know that I am in the midst of Israel,
And that I am the Lord your God
And there is no other;
And my people will never be put to shame.

(Joel 2:18–27 NAS)

I believe in revival, the kind of revival Joel talks about. I believe God wants to give us another spiritual awakening. I believe before our Lord returns to write the final chapter of history, he will be preceded by a great, spiritual awakening. I believe that praying for revival is like waiting for the sun to rise: you can't speed it up, but it does come up – you don't wait in vain.

Deliverance Through Intercession and Fasting

The examples we've looked at so far have been for the most part, examples of personal deliverance. But God uses intercession and fasting to bring about the deliverance of *others* also. Let me cite three incidents.

In Ezra 10:6, we read 'Then Ezra rose from before the house of God and went into the chamber of Jehohanan the son of Eliashib. Although he went there, he did not eat bread, nor drink water, for he was mourning over the unfaithfulness of the exiles' (NAS). While in exile the people had broken God's commandment by intermarrying, and Ezra's grief over their sin expresses itself through fasting. The result was that the people confessed their sin and abandoned the practice of intermarriage.

Another example of intercession and fasting is found in Nehemiah chapter 1. This man of God prays for his backsliding people. 'Now it came about when I heard

139

these words, I sat down and wept and mourned for days; and I was fasting and praying before the God of heaven. And I said, "I beseech thee, O Lord God of heaven . . . let thine ear now be attentive and thine eye open to hear the prayer of thy servant which I am praying before thee now, day and night, on behalf of the sons of Israel thy servants, confessing the sins of the sons of Israel which we have sinned against thee; I and my father's house have sinned"' (Nehemiah 1:4–6).

No greater illustration of delivering others through prayer and fasting exists than that of Moses. Perhaps he more than any other besides Jesus, knew what it meant to stand in the gap between a holy God and a sinful people. Before he died, Moses laid down the reins and reminded Israel of his intercession for them.

> And I fell down before the Lord, as at the first, forty days and nights; I neither ate bread nor drank water, because of all your sin which you had committed in doing what was evil in the sight of the Lord to provoke him to anger. For I was afraid of the anger and hot displeasure with which the Lord was wrathful against you in order to destroy you *but the Lord listened to me that time also*. And the Lord was angry enough with Aaron to destroy him; *so I also prayed for Aaron at the same time* (Deuteronomy 9:18–20 NAS, emphasis added).

Think of it: Just *one* man, paying the price in fasting and intercession, and an entire nation delivered from judgment. Do we even dare guess what might take place in our homes and schools and churches, *in our world*, if Christians awakened to their right and responsibility to wield such power through prayer and fasting? Can you envision the unending procession of liberated lives streaming out of darkness into the Kingdom of Light? Can you see Satan cower in defeat as hundreds of intercessors invade his citadel and set free the captives of sin?

The Rewards of Fasting

Jesus said, 'But you, when you fast, anoint your head, and wash your face so that you may not be seen fasting by men, but by your Father who is in secret; and your Father who sees in secret will repay you' (Matthew 6:17,18 NAS). Jesus did not consider rewards too low a motive to mention, and along with acts of charity and prayer, he promised a reward would be given to those who fasted in the proper spirit. In verse 16 he mentions the reward of those who fast in order to impress others with their piety. 'Truly I say to you, they have their reward in full' (NAS).

The word Jesus uses for reward in verse 16 is different from the one used in verse 18. The word used to describe the reward of the hypocrite implies an *immediate reward* and a *reward paid in full*. In other words, 'What you see is what you get.' But the word Jesus uses to describe the reward given in response to the right spirit suggests a restoration over a period of time. The rewards of fasting are like dividends from blue-chip stock. Day after day, God continues to unfold for you and others the rewards of fasting.

10: A Praying Church in a Pagan World

It is reported that Mary, Queen of Scots, once said, 'I fear the prayers of John Knox more than I fear all the armies on the face of the earth'.

That was probably the last time anyone feared the prayers of the church.

It's hard to picture Yasser Arafat saying, 'I fear the prayers of the saints more than I fear all the Uzis of Israel'.

The world does not fear the church – it barely tolerates it. Generally, the world perceives the church as no longer a player in world affairs, only an observer, a 'Yes-man' for the pagan leaders of Western culture, a culture that has long since abandoned Christian presuppositions as a serious voice in shaping the values of modern society. The church is a quaint relic of the past that lends a certain charm to the neighbourhood, a holdover from bygone days, big but harmless, like a beached whale.

For many the most crucial question facing the church is whether it can survive. I can answer that question. Yes, the church will survive. God has never left himself without a witness, and his church will still be around when the curtain comes down on this whole mess.

Rest assured, the church will survive. Perhaps not in its present form, but it will survive. But God help us if we're interested only in surviving. Christ intends that his church do a lot more than merely survive. And that's what this chapter is about.

'The Post-Christian age is here.' These are the opening words of Harold Lindsell's book, *The New Paganism.* The purpose of his book is to show that the Western world has been overcome by paganism. And he succeeds. Lindsell writes: 'In the West the civilization based on Judeo–Christian foundations has collapsed. In its place the West without exception now lives and functions as a pagan world.'[2] Which means that the church here and everywhere else is treading water in a sea of paganism. It is surrounded by a hostile world that is opposed to New Testament Christianity and against which it wages an unrelenting war.

Some reject the term 'paganism', preferring instead 'secular humanism' or 'neo-paganism'. The difference is academic. Whatever we call it, one thing is clear: our generation has witnessed the final death blows to the Judeo–Christian foundation upon which much of the Western world was established.

I can remember when the Christian ethic was a given in our society. It was the standard, more or less, by which both Christian and non-Christian operated. Even in Hollywood. Remember when the old Hayes office set a time limit on screen kisses? No sex outside marriage? Husband and wife shown in twin beds only, and the good guy always won? I remember when Clark Gable shocked theatre-goers with a mild four-letter expletive in the final scene of *Gone With the Wind*. People *gasped*. Really, they did. Now I hear preachers use worse words than that from the pulpit.

A grotesque example of this new paganism appeared in a recent newspaper article:

BALTIMORE – Health workers are counting used condoms that float to the surface of the city's sewage treatment plant pools in an effort to find out how many people are heeding advice about safe sex to avoid infection with the AIDS virus.

Hundreds of condoms float in the water at open-air pools at waste water treatment plants.

For eight months, city workers have been using long-handled fish nets to scoop the multicoloured condoms from the sewage each day.[3]

We used to sin in retail, now we do it wholesale. Having rejected any transcendent frame of reference, we have become volume dealers in unrighteousness, while everyone does that which is right in their own eyes.

The only hope for our society is that the church will recapture its distinctiveness, act instead of react, get off the defensive and take the offensive, and stop letting the world set its agenda.

The operative word here is *distinctiveness*. Webster's dictionary has this entry under the word *distinct*:

1. Not alike; different.
2. Not the same; separate; individual.
3. Clearly marked off; clear; plain.
4. Well-defined; unmistakable; definite.

That sounds a lot like the word *holy*, which Christians are supposed to be. The effectiveness of the church depends absolutely upon its distinctiveness. And to the degree that we have lost that distinctiveness, we have lost our influence for Christ in the world. The more the church looks like the world, talks like the world, operates like the world, the more the world disdains it, for the world can beat the church at everything – except this: living out the life of Christ. That and that alone is our distinctiveness, and in that and that alone lies our power.

Christ could not have made this any clearer than he did when he called us 'salt' and 'light'. There is no greater contrast than that of light and darkness – except one: the church and the world. Circle the globe and you'll find Christians everywhere, in every society, in every culture.

144

The question must be asked: with all this light why is the world so dark? With all this salt why is society so rotten?

The prevailing climate is nothing new to the church. It was born in the midst of paganism, and conquered it. 'Three hundred years after the beginning of Christ's public ministry the church had brought the Roman Empire to its knees in worship of the Redeemer.'[4]

How did they do it? How did that little band of eager disciples accomplish what no military power had been able to? Did they possess something that we do not? Did they know something that we do not?

The answer to those questions and others can be found in the record God has preserved of those pioneer Christians. A more revealing picture of the life and times of the early church can't be found than the one in Acts Chapter 12.

The chapter opens with a bang:

> Now about that time Herod the king stretched out his hand to harass some from the church. Then he killed James the brother of John with the sword. And because he saw that it pleased the Jews, he proceeded further to seize Peter also. Now it was during the Days of Unleavened Bread (Acts 12:1–3).

Herod assigned sixteen soldiers to guard Peter, and he was bound by chains between two of them. For Peter there would be no escape, no reprieve.

'But constant prayer was offered to God for him by the church' (verse 5).

The night before Peter was to be executed an angel appeared in the prison where Peter was sleeping between two guards. The angel kicked Peter and told him to wake up and get dressed. As the chains fell off Peter, he put on his sandals and his garment and followed the heavenly visitor past the two guard posts, through the iron gate of the city, which opened automatically, and into a street, where the angel vanished as suddenly as he had appeared.

And when Peter had come to himself, he said, 'Now I know for certain that the Lord has sent his angel, and has delivered me from the expectation of the Jewish people'.

So when he had considered this, he came to the house of Mary, the mother of John whose surname was Mark, where many were gathered together praying (Verses 11, 12).

Why didn't he run away? This panic-prone disciple had run away before – when Jesus was on trial. He has a better excuse now. His life *really is* in danger. But instead of fleeing he goes to Mary's house where he knows the church is gathered. Later he will go into hiding but first he must share with the church what God has done. Throughout the entire story (verses 1–19) we are struck by the remarkably calm control exercised by this former deserter.

The clue is in the words of verse twelve: 'So, *when he had considered this*, he came to the house of Mary . . .' Peter has matured; he stops and thinks before he runs. He considers what has just happened to him, then courageously and calmly goes to church.

The word 'considered' means *to see together*. Peter took the recent events and put them together; he saw them as a whole, not as isolated, unrelated happenings. If he had looked only at the death of James, he might have fled; if he had looked only at the chains and the guards, he might have panicked as before. He now understood that everything in life is tied to something else. No event occurs in isolation. Every thread is part of the same fabric.

The same is true of us today. Many of the doom and gloom assessments of the church's status are the result of seeing things in isolation from other things. I believe Christians need to consider, 'to see together', all the happenings in our world. When we do we shall begin to become the 'church optimistic' as well as the 'church militant'. I suggest that we consider, 'see together', four facts.

1. The church and the world are deadly enemies

The old Isaac Watts hymn asked the question, 'Is this vile world a friend of grace, to help me on to God?' The answer was 'no' then, and it's still 'no'. The early church knew this. I'm not sure we do. I think many still hope we can make up and become friends, or at least live in peaceful co-existence as good neighbours.

I grew up in the Baptist church, and in those days Baptists were pretty strict when it came to worldly pleasures. We kids used to sing, 'I don't smoke and I don't chew, and I don't go with girls that do.' Anyway, I was trying to get my mother's permission to go to a dance, which was one of the major taboos. Patiently, she tried to explain to me the great gulf between worldly pleasure and the Christian (Baptist) faith.

That was when I made my first attempt to join the worship of Jehovah and the worship of Baal. 'How about if we dance to "The Old Rugged Cross"?'

I'll never forget the look she gave me.

The enmity between the church and the world is enunciated by the apostle John when he says:

Do not love the world or the things in the world. If anyone loves the world, the love of the Father is not in him.

For all that is in the world – the lust of the flesh, the lust of the eyes, and the pride of life – is not of the Father but is of the world.

And the world is passing away, and the lust of it; but he who does the will of God abides for ever (I John 2:15–17).

John uses the word 'world' more often than all the other New Testament writers combined – seventy-nine times in the gospel and twenty-three times in the first epistle. The world that we are to shun is not the world of nature, the created order, the material universe, nor is it the world of people, the human race, the world as a fallen world in need of grace. It is the world as a system organised without God, the unbelieving, pagan society, a society embodying the influences and forces hostile to God. This world about which John warns us 'is not made up of so many outward objects that can be specified; it is the sum of those influences emanating from men and things around us, which draw away from God. It is the awful down-dragging current in life.'[5] The world is human civilisation organised and operating under the power of evil.

There's another aspect to this first fact that needs to be noted: the enemies of Christ always unite. When Herod killed James with the sword, he saw that it pleased the Jews, so he took steps to kill Peter also. Herod's actions were not motivated by great principles or deep convictions, but by a sorry desire to win the popularity of the Jews. The Jews were never fond of the Herods; they were usurpers and Edomite blood flowed in their veins. But this Herod, Herod Agrippa, grandson of Herod the Great, courted the Jews by keeping the Law and all the Jewish observances, even to the point of delaying Peter's execution until after the Passover. Herod and the Jews united against the church. Peter was killed by public opinion as much as by the sword.

This persecution under Herod Agrippa I was the third major attack on the apostles. The first was led by the Sadducees and the next by the Pharisees (Acts 4, 8).

The Pharisees and the Sadducees were cat-and-dog enemies. The Sadducees (the righteous ones) did not believe in the resurrection of the body or life after death and reject rabbinic interpretation of the law.

The Pharisees (the separate ones) were legalists, concerned with ritual purity, tithing and strict observance of the law. But while these two groups were divided against each other they were united against Christ (Matthew 16:1f; 22:15-34). In Matthew 22:34, we read, 'But when the Pharisees heard that he had silenced the Sadducees, they gathered together.'

During Jesus' trial, when Pilate learned that Jesus was from Galilee, he sent him to Herod Antipas, who was ruler of Galilee and Peraea, and had jurisdiction over the Man from Galilee. Herod, after playing with Jesus, mocking him and treating him with contempt, sent him back to Pilate. Luke adds this footnote to the incident: 'That very day Pilate and Herod became friends with each other, for before that they had been at enmity with each other' (Luke 23:12).

A parallel in our day is how the *isms* have united against Christianity. Secularism has united with humanism, giving us secular humanism, liberalism has joined pluralism, Hedonism has blended into existentialism, and atheism has joined them all. To some, the isms may be nothing but abstract terms that have nothing to do with everyday life. Understandable – the postman and I hardly ever discuss existentialism, and I can't remember the last time I chit-chatted with someone about pluralism or relativism.

But what all this means basically is that every major idea and philosophy shaping our world right now is opposed to New Testament Christianity and means to wipe it from the face of the earth.

The church has imbibed more of these philosophies than it realises and much of its message and ministry is becoming an ism in sheep's clothing.

2. The success of evil is only apparent

For years Walter Cronkite ended his CBS news report with the words: 'And that's the way it is.' A more accurate statement would have been: 'And that's the way it *appears*.'

Here is where 'seeing together' is crucial. If you isolate the death of James and view it as a single, independent and unrelated event, you say, 'Evil wins again. Once again God was out-manoevured by the devil.' But when you gather everything together and see everything together, you know differently. If God delivered Peter, then he could have delivered James, therefore, it only looked like God had been out-manoeuvered.

Of course, this is one of the great tests of our faith, a test we do not always pass. Like the Psalmist, when we see the prosperity of the wicked who 'have more than heart could wish', we feel like saying, 'Surely I have cleansed my heart in vain, and washed my hands in innocence' (Psalm 71:1, 7, 13). There is only one cure for this: 'when I thought how to understand this, it was too painful for me – *until I went into the sanctuary of God: then I understood their end*' (Psalm 73:16, 17 emphasis added).

Listen to God as he speaks to our anxious hearts: 'Do not fret because of evil men or be envious of those who do wrong; for like the grass they will soon wither, like green plants they will soon die away . . . Do not fret when men succeed in their ways, when they carry out their wicked schemes . . . for evil men will be cut off . . . a little while, and the wicked will be no more; though you look for them, they will not be found. But the meek will inherit the land and enjoy great peace' (Psalm 37:1, 2, 7, 10 NIV).

Just as the guards looked for Peter and could not find him, the day is coming when we will look for the wicked and be unable to find them. When the upright get uptight they need to remember: the success of evil is only apparent.

3. God's hand, though unseen, is working

We cannot always accurately interpret our situation; often outside circumstances contradict everything we believe. It is impossible to evaluate a situation on the basis of visible evidence. Like Philip, when asked by Jesus how they could feed the five thousand, we dig into the pockets of our own resources, and come up blank (John 6:5).[6]

Our God is often a silent and hidden God. Witness the unseen hand of God. The angel appears in the prison – the guards do not see him. A light illuminates the cell – the guards do not see it. The angel strikes Peter in the side, the chains fall off, but the guards do not hear the clatter of chains falling on stone. Peter straps on his sandals and clomps out of prison – the guards do not hear. Peter was long delivered before the guards realised he was gone.

For that matter, Peter was delivered before he realised it. It was only after stepping into the street that he 'came to himself' and knew he had been delivered.

4. The unseen hand of God is moved by prayer

The response of the church to Peter's imprisonment is stated in verse 5: 'Peter was therefore kept in prison, *but constant prayer was offered to God for him by the church.*' The author of Acts would have us know that there was a vital connection between the deliverance of Peter and the prayers of the church.

I hesitate to say that God's hand *is moved by prayer*, because it almost sounds like I am infringing upon God's sovereignty. But in light of what we have already covered in the first two chapters, I think the wording is legitimate. Prayer does move the hand of God.

Instead of casting prayer as a polite nod to tradition, a piece of pietistic irrelevance, we must see it as the true power of the church. The early church didn't have enough influence or prestige to get Peter out of prison, but they had enough power to pray him out. And even they did not know how strong they were, not believing Peter was standing at the door knocking.

The church has far more power than it knows. Much is being said and written today about the desperate need for an evangelical awakening like the one that came to England in the late eighteenth century under John Wesley. It was the influence of John Wesley and the Evangelical Revival, say historians, that spared England from a bloody revolution like the one that tore France apart.

J. Edwin Orr in his remarkable book, *The Eager Feet*, tells of the Concert of Prayer started by the Baptist Association of the Midlands, joined by members of the Free Church, Methodists, Anglicans and other burdened believers. This Concert of Prayer paved the way not only for the general awakening, but also for the extraordinary outburst of missionary zeal in the last decade of the eighteenth century, 'It is significant,' writes Orr, 'that the union in prayer for a general revival preceded the French Revolution by a full seven years. The prevenient work of the Holy Spirit has often anticipated the onslaught of Evil long before believers had become aware of the dangers that lay ahead.'[7]

In his book, *England Before and After Wesley*, J. Wesley Bready comes to the conclusion that the 'Evangelical Awakening was the true nursing-mother of the spirit and character values that have created and sustained free institutions throughout the English-speaking world.' Bready calls it 'the moral watershed of Anglo-Saxon history.'[8]

For most of my ministry I have been a student of revival and awakening and I have constantly run into one stubborn fact: in the recorded history of the church there has never been a mighty outpouring of the Spirit in revival that did not begin in the persistent, prevailing prayers of desperate people. Revival has never come because men placed it on the calendar. It has come because God placed it in their hearts.

What could we expect to happen if the church returned to its kneeling posture and recovered its prayer power. We have seen one picture of the church in Acts 12, now let's focus on the praying church in Acts 4.

The apostles have just had their first head-on collision with the Sanhedrin, a confrontation brought about by the healing of a lame man (Acts 3). When the people saw the former cripple walking, leaping and praising God, they mobbed Peter and John; Peter seized the opportunity to preach Christ to them. As he was telling the people that Jesus, who had been crucified, had been raised from the grave and was truly both Lord and Christ, the priests and Sadducees, angered by the apostle's talk of resurrection, grabbed them and threw them in jail.

The next day, the Sanhedrin, after threatening Peter and John, commanded them not to speak or teach in the name of Jesus, and released them from custody. Immediately, the two disciples returned to the gathered believers and related the story. And what was the young church's reaction?

Did they try to establish a dialogue with the Sanhedrin or organise a protest march against religious discrimination? No, this young body of believers, faced with its first opposition, went to its knees.

What happened when the church prayed is recorded in verse 31: 'And when they had prayed, the place where they were assembled together was shaken; and they were all filled with the Holy Spirit, and they spoke the word of God with boldness.'

The presence of God perceived

'The place was shaken.' This expression symbolises God's active presence. A similar phrase occurs in Acts 16:26. In Philippi, Paul and Silas had been beaten and thrown into prison with their feet fastened in stocks. But at midnight the two missionaries began to pray and sing hymns, and 'suddenly there was a great earthquake, so that the foundations of the prison were shaken; and immediately all the doors were opened and everyone's chains were loosed.' This is the manifestation of God's presence, declaring that he is there and that he is acting.

But isn't God always present when two or three gather in his name? That is true, but God can be present without our knowledge of it. At Bethel, after seeing the manifestation of God in the angels ascending and descending on a ladder stretching from earth to heaven, Jacob said, 'Surely the Lord is in this place, and I did not know it' (Genesis 28:16). That could be the theme song of many a Sunday morning worship service.

We do always have the presence of God. What we do not always have, however, is the awareness of his presence. Vance Havner used to say that when we preachers look out upon our small remnant and quote, 'Where two or three are gathered together in my name, there am I in the midst of them,' we are usually more conscious of the absence of the people than the presence of the Lord.

God's presence isn't real to us. We speak of him as though he were absent. We pray that way. Have you ever listened to prayers, to your own prayers? We speak of God in the third person, as though we were talking to the congregation rather than praying to God.

But when the church abandons itself to prayer, the presence of God is perceived. Suddenly we know he is there, working, moving, answering.

And that is enough. Enough to know he is on the scene. Let the Sanhedrin rant and rave, let them threaten, let them condemn, God is with us and that is enough. In the face of insurmountable difficulties the assurance of his presence is sufficient.

This perceived presence – an atmosphere charged with the obvious presence of God in such a way people know he is there – is a common characteristic of great revivals.

During the Welsh revival it was reported that strangers, unaware of the awakening, coming into the villages would suddenly fall under deep conviction and seek out a minister to pray for them. Fishermen, drawing near to shore, again unaware of the revival, would come under terrible conviction of sin and before their feet touched shore everyone on board would be converted.

It was said of Charles Finney that during times of revival he could walk down a street and passers-by would literally be thrown to their knees under the weight of conviction. But everywhere Finney went, a man called Father Nash accompanied him and closeted himself in a room to do nothing but intercede for Finney and the meetings.

I have witnessed this 'atmospheric revival' a few times – times when the presence of God was 'so thick you could cut it with a knife', as one student expressed it. People driving on to the church parking lot and falling immediately under conviction, people calling in the middle of the night, unable to wait until morning, asking how to be saved, people making restitution and seeking reconciliation – all these things and more.

In the early 1950s this kind of revival came to our city, under the ministry of my home church and its pastor. Everywhere I went in town, on a city bus, in the park, at school, I heard people talking about it. Not all good talk, but talk. You couldn't escape the confrontation. It was said that to escape the 'atmosphere' you had to get at least a hundred miles away. As a teenager, I remember standing on the steps outside the church, praying and confessing my sins. I wasn't about to walk in there without being right with God.

It would be a mistake to take these, or any examples, and make them the 'norm' for God's manifestation. I've been in some churches that shook, not by the presence of God, but by loud preaching and blaring amplifiers. Shaking buildings is not our business, nor is it our task to produce signs of his presence. When the Lord shakes the building you do not have to announce it.

In extraordinary times God does extraordinary things. But God is as much in the ordinary as he is in the extraordinary. The same God who raised Jesus from the grave is the same God who raises the sun every morning.

One thing: the Bible says this praying church 'raised their voice to God with one accord' (verse 2). This is an eloquent statement of the church's oneness, both in their action and their motive. It wasn't just the apostles who prayed. They all prayed. Here was a group of believers who gathered in one place to do one thing with one motive. This is a testimony to united prayer.

While there is power in the prayers of one person, the Bible indicates there is something special about united prayer. Jesus said, 'Again I say to you that if two of you agree on earth concerning anything that they ask, it will be done for them by my Father in heaven' (Matthew 18:19).

The church was in one accord, like the men of Israel who came together to make David king: 'All these men of war, who could keep ranks, came to Hebron with a loyal heart, to make David king over all Israel; and all the rest of Israel were of one mind to make David king' (1 Chronicles 12:38).

That is the kind of praying that shakes the place – when God's people come together with one heart to make Jesus king. When all our different concerns are thrust aside and our hearts flow into one main stream – that's when the presence of God is manifested and people know God has taken the field.

The Power of God Received

'And when they prayed . . . they were all filled with the Holy Spirit' (verse 31). They were *all* filled, the record states. Not the apostles only, but every member of the church experienced the Spirit's filling. There had been such a filling on the day of Pentecost but the church can't run on the fumes of a previous fill-up. Every new task demands a fresh fullness.

There is something remarkable about this incident. As a result of their praying, they were all filled with the Holy Spirit – but examine the prayer. The Holy Spirit isn't mentioned; to be filled with the Spirit was not part of the petition. They didn't pray to be filled with the Spirit but when they prayed they were filled with the Spirit. Two things are significant.

One, they were not seeking an experience. There was nothing selfish or subjective about their petition. They weren't after the 'thrill of the fill'. I have witnessed a strange transition during my ministry. It used to be that Christians wanted the fullness of the Spirit for power – power to serve Christ and power to live for him. But now we act as though the purpose of being filled is not power in serving, but pleasure in living. The goal of it all is to feel good and have tremendous ecstatic experiences. I'm afraid many of us are more interested in the 'feeling of the Spirit' than the filling of the Spirit.

In the second place these verses show that there is more to being filled with the Spirit than merely asking for it. As a matter of fact, we don't have to ask God to fill us in order to be filled. The New Testament doesn't tell of anyone actually asking to be filled with the Spirit. Luke 11:13 comes close.* I am not saying we ought not to pray to be filled. We can, but it isn't necessary. If we examine the content of their prayer we may discover the kind of praying that results in the filling of the Spirit.

---

* 'If you then, being evil, know how to give good gifts to your children, how much more will your heavenly Father give the Holy Spirit to those who ask him!'

1. They Recognised God as Sovereign

In Acts 4 verse 24 we read, 'So when they heard that, they raised their voice to God with one accord and said: "Lord, you are God, who made heaven and earth and the sea, and all that is in them."'

The word translated 'Lord' here is rare. It is not the same word rendered 'Lord' in verse 29. This word (verse 24) is an extremely strong word meaning 'despot', one who rules with absolute and unrestrained authority. Omnipotence is in the word.

This is where they started – not with the threats of the enemy but with the absolute authority of God. For the church, victory always begins with the recognition that God is our Sovereign Lord.

His sovereignty is seen in the creation of all things. They acknowledged God as the creator of heaven and earth and the sea, 'and all that is in them'. Why? Because they had a problem with some of the 'all that is in them'. The Sanhedrin were creatures and God created them. They looked beyond the creation to the creator, beyond the visible to the invisible. One of the favourite threats kids use with each other is, 'I'm going to tell on you!' Well, that's what these Christians did – they told on the Sanhedrin. Part of the creation was troubling them and they appealed to the Creator.

His sovereignty is also seen in his control of all things. Look again at their prayer. They began by quoting from Psalm 2.

Verses 26 and 27: '"The kings of the earth took their stand, and the rulers were gathered together against the Lord and against His Christ."

For truly against your holy Servant Jesus, whom you anointed, both Herod and Pontius Pilate, with the Gentiles and the people of Israel were gathered together . . .'

Look at the powers gathered against Christ – kings and rulers, Herod and Pilate, the Gentiles and Israel.

But that's not the end. They go on,

'To do whatever your hand and your purpose determined before to be done' (verse 28).

These persecuted believers looked back at the darkest day of their lives, the day their hopes and dreams disintegrated with the death of Christ, and saw *God in charge of it all*. And if it was true with the crucifixion of their Lord, how much more so with the persecution of his disciples. That was a magnificent display of his absolute sovereignty.

2. They recognised themselves as God's servants

In verse 29 they refer to themselves as servants, bond-slaves.

'Now, Lord, look on their threats, and grant to your servants *that with all boldness they may speak your word*' (emphasis added).

This was a prayer of submission. They didn't complain about the circumstances or call down fire from heaven on the Sanhedrin. Nor did they beg God to move them to a more favourable situation. They simply asked God for more of what had gotten them into trouble in the first place – boldness ('Now when they saw the boldness of Peter and John . . . 'Acts 4:13). They submitted to the God-allowed circumstances.

They also submitted to their God-appointed commission. They prayed, 'Now, Lord, look on their threats, and grant to your servants that with all boldness *they may speak your word*' (verse 29, emphasis added).

The plea of the prayer is that they will have the boldness to continue doing what God had called them to do – speaking the word and glorifying Jesus.

Now let's put it all together. In their prayer which brought about a fresh supply of the power of God, they, *one*, acknowledged God as the sovereign Lord and, *two*, submitted to him and his redemptive purpose. I believe it is safe to say that any Christian who acknowledges and submits to the Lordship of Jesus Christ is filled with the Holy Spirit.

When the Holy Spirit finds a believer who wants what he wants, they 'get together'. The Spirit is interested in one thing – glorifying Jesus as Lord and Saviour. And he is ready to fill any Christian through whom he can do that.

The Purpose of God Achieved

Verse 33 contains two noteworthy phrases: 'great power' and 'great grace'. This band of believers possessed 'great power' to *do* what God wanted and 'great grace' to *be* what God wanted – an empowered witness and an enriched life.

An Empowered Witness

'And they spoke the word of God with boldness' (verse 31). Notice the chain reaction here: when a church is filled with the Holy Spirit it will inevitably speak the word of God with boldness. We cannot divorce the fullness of the Spirit from witnessing. To be filled with the Spirit is to allow the Holy Spirit to express himself through us, to carry out his commission through our lives. And unless we are willing to be instruments of his purpose it is useless to pray for his help.

Witnesses are not made by training programmes. Training programmes can teach us how to witness, but only the compelling power of the Holy Spirit can make us witnesses.

When I use the term 'witness' I am not referring to any particular method of witnessing. I don't mean that if you're filled with the Holy Spirit you will preach on street corners – you may or you may not. It is for the Spirit to say how, when and where we witness; but our

160

lives, in one way or another, will witness of the Lord Jesus Christ when we are yielded to the Spirit.

It is worth our time to mark some of the features of this witness.

With great power the apostles 'gave' witness. The word translated 'gave' means to give back, to return; it conveys the idea of repaying a debt or fulfilling an obligation. We are not doing God a favour when we share Christ with others. We are repaying a debt. It is something we are obligated to do. The Holy Spirit makes a man honest, and an honest man always repays his debts. Paul expressed this same sense of obligation to the Romans (Romans 1:14).

They spoke the word of God with 'boldness'. Boldness is one of the great words of the New Testament. Again and again God uses this word to characterise the lives and ministries of New Testament believers. As used in the New Testament, boldness contains three shades of meaning.

(1) It means courage to speak, especially in the presence of men of high rank. The immediate example of this, of course, is the transformation of Peter from that of the cowering Christ-denier to the fearless preacher of Pentecost. In churches across the country I have asked Christians the main problem they have with witnessing to a lost person. The leading answer is always fear. But the Spirit gives us the courage to speak.

(2) It means clarity of speech, the ability to make clear and plain the message of Christ. The Holy Spirit can give us the ability to express ourselves, to make our witness understood.

(3) It means confidence in what we speak. This is the heart-assurance that what we say will be driven home by the Spirit. Though we may see no visible signs, we know our words penetrate the heart and the seed of the gospel is sown.

What was this witness that they gave with great power? It was the resurrection. 'And with great power the apostles gave witness to the resurrection of the Lord Jesus'(verse 33). Our message is that Jesus is living and that he is Lord. And this brings us back to where we started. When the place is shaken and the presence of God is perceived, it's not difficult to convince men that Jesus is both living and Lord. When the Philippian jailer, standing amid the rubble of his demolished jail, saw the prison doors hanging on broken hinges, heard Paul and Silas singing hymns and praising God, and saw that all the prisoners were still there, he was convinced and cried out, 'What must I do to be saved?' (Acts 16:25–30). He wasn't a prospect for the God-is-Dead movement – he had perceived the presence of God.

It is hard to convince an atheistic age like ours to believe that Jesus is alive and reigning if they see little evidence to support our claim. At Pentecost, Peter pointed to the manifestation of the Holy Spirit as proof that Jesus was both Lord and Christ, sitting at the right hand of God (Acts 2:33).

An Enriched life

'And great grace was upon them all' (verse 33). Can you think of a more eloquent description of this community of unity?

A part of this 'great grace' was surely the harmony of the fellowship described by the phrase, 'one heart and one soul' (verse 32). Many believers but one body, beating with one heart, thinking with one mind, feeling with one soul. The most ignorant sinner in town knows that the mark of Christianity is unity. It is precisely this, Jesus said, that shows the world that the Father sent him: 'That they all may be one, as you, Father, are in me, and I in you; that they also may be one in us, that the world may believe that you sent me' (John 17:21).

Another part of the 'great grace' that was upon the church is expressed in these words: 'Neither did anyone say that any of the things he possessed was his own, but they had all things in common . . . Nor was there anyone among them who lacked; for all who were possessors of lands or houses sold them, and brought the proceeds of the things that were sold, and laid them at the apostles' feet; and they distributed to each as anyone had need' (verses 32, 34, 35).

This is what happens to a praying church: the Holy Spirit baptises it with a new concept, a changed viewpoint. The members have a new sense of responsibility toward one another, and they see their possessions as a trust given by God to be used as needed among the family. Did you know there was no such thing as a 'needy person' in that church? 'There were no needy persons among them,' reads the NIV.

Party causes, petty claims, little ownerships and narrow boundaries were carried away by the flow of the Spirit, and hand joined heart as the church cared for both the spiritual and the social needs of one another. And, in reality, the two cannot be severed, for the witness of one makes believeable the witness of the other. The twin spirals of smoke ascending to the Father come from the same sweet-smelling sacrifice.

Joseph Parker depicted a church that has lost this spirit: 'The building stands there of undiminished magnitude and undimmed beauty of forms and colour . . . but GOD has gone . . . The very self-same old hymns were sung that fifty years ago caused the walls to vibrate as with conscious joy; and though the music was exact in technicality, and well performed as to mere lip service, the old passion was not there, and the hymn rose to the ceiling, bruised itself against the beams of the roof, and fell back, a service unrecognised in heaven.'

It may look as though I have painted this church in unrealistic colours – and I admit it does sound like the

First Baptist Church of Eden – but if I continued into Acts chapter 5 I would have to use darker colours. The church portrayed in Acts was by no means perfect, nor did Luke intend to present it as such, but its imperfections were not *conspicuous*, and therein lies the vital difference. Because it was a praying church the most conspicuous thing about it was Christ.

The Church must learn to live in a kneeling position, for there can be no praying for revival until there is a revival of praying.

Notes

Chapter One

1. Barnabas Lindars, *The New Century Bible, The Gospel of John* (Grand Rapids: Wm. B. Eerdmans Publishing Company, 1972), p. 475.
2. Quoted by Leon Morris, *The New International Commentary, The Gospel of John* (Grand Rapids: Wm. B. Eerdmans Publishing Company, 1971), p. 646.
3. *ibid*, p. 646.
4. Curtis C. Mitchell, *Praying Jesus' Way* (Old Tappan: Fleming H. Revell Company, 1977), p. 139.
5. From an interview, February 1969.

Chapter Two

1. F. W. Robertson, *Sermons Preached at Brighton* (New York: Harper & Row, 1988), p. 644.
2. Curtis C. Mitchell, *Praying Jesus' Way* (Old Tappan: Fleming H. Revell Company, 1977), p. 11.
3. Ernst Kasemann, *Commentary on Romans* (Grand Rapids: Wm. B. Eerdmans Publishing Company, 1980), p. 292.

Chapter Four

1. Alexander MacLaren, *Expositions of Holy Scripture* Vol. 2 (Grand Rapids: Wm. B. Eerdmans Publishing Company, 1959 Reprint), p. 172.

Chapter Five

1. Lewis B. Smedes, *How Can It Be All Right When Everything Is All Wrong?* (San Francisco: Harper & Row Publishers , 1982), p. 63.

2. Karl Barth, quoted by Jacobus J. Muller, *The Epistles of Paul to the Philippians and Philemon*, The New International Commentary on the New Testament (Grand Rapids: Wm. B. Eerdmans Publishing Company, 1955), p. 57.

3. John Stott, *Involvement: Being A Responsible Christian in a non-Christian Society* (Old Tappan: Fleming H. Revell Company, 1984), p. 105.

Chapter Six

1. Lewis Sperry Chafer, *True Evangelism* (Findlay, Ohio: The Dunham Publishing Company, 1919), pp. 3, 4.

2. John Eadie, *Thessalonians: A Commentary on the Greek Text* (Grand Rapids: Baker Book House, no date), p. 203.

3. For a discussion of this see, *Faith That Will Not Fail*, by Ronald Dunn (Basingstoke, UK: Marshall Pickering, 1987), pp. 56–60.

4. S. D. Gordon, *Quiet Talks on Prayer* (Old Tappan: Fleming H. Revell Company, 1967 Reprint), p. 132.

Chapter Eight

1. C. S. Lewis, *A Grief Observed* (New York: The Seabury Press, 1963), pp. 4, 5.

Chapter Ten

1. Harold Lindsell, *The New Paganism* (San Francisco: Harper & Row Publishers, 1987), p. x.

2. *Ibid*, p. 213.

3. *Dallas Times Herald*, 15 April 1988.

4. Lindsell, *Op. cit*. p. 22.

5. George C. Findlay, *Fellowship in the Life Eternal* (Grand Rapids: Wm. B. Eerdmans Publishing Company, 1955 Reprint), p. 199.

6. For a discussion of this aspect of faith, see *Faith That Will Not Fail*, by Ronald Dunn, (Basingstoke, UK: Marshall Pickering, 1987), pp. 66–79.

7. J. Edwin Orr, *The Eager Feet* (Chicago: Moody Press, 1975), p. 15.

8. J. Wesley Bready, *England: Before and After Wesley* (Sevenoaks, UK: Hodder & Stoughton, 1939), p. 11, 14.